MARY'S GRAMMAR

MARY'S GRAMMAR

BY

JANE MARCET

YESTERDAY'S CLASSICS

CHAPEL HILL, NORTH CAROLINA

This edition, first published in 2011 by Yesterday's Classics, an imprint of Yesterday's Classics, LLC, is an unabridged republication of the text originally published by Longman, Brown, Green, & Longmans in 1848. For the complete listing of the books that are published by Yesterday's Classics, please visit www.yesterdaysclassics.com. Yesterday's Classics is the publishing arm of the Baldwin Online Children's Literature Project which presents the complete text of hundreds of classic books for children at www.mainlesson.com.

ISBN-10: 1-59915-390-4

ISBN-13: 978-1-59915-390-2

Yesterday's Classics, LLC
PO Box 3418
Chapel Hill, NC 27515

PREFACE

I have so often pitied children who have been studying a grammar which they did not understand, that I thought I could not do them a better service than endeavour to render so dry and abstruse a subject easy and familiar. In the elucidation of the first elements of grammar, I hope my attempt has not entirely failed; but had I been aware of the *metaphysical* difficulties I should have to encounter in a further development of the subject, I do not think I should have undertaken the task. It is true, that the consideration of such difficulties seldom occurs to the minds of children, and may, perhaps, without inconvenience be disregarded in a work intended for them alone. They form, however, an insuperable obstacle to my rendering this little work as clear and intelligible as might be wished; and will, I trust, afford some apology for its imperfections.

The stories have been introduced with the view of amusing children during the prosecution of so dry a study; but they may occasionally be used with advantage as parsing exercises.

CONTENTS

PART I

PART II

LESSON I

NOUNS

A LITTLE girl was sitting one day with a book in her hand which she was studying with a woe-begone countenance, when her mother came into the room. "Why, Mary!" said her mother, "what is the matter? Your book is not very entertaining, I fear."

"No, indeed it is not," replied the child, who could scarcely help crying; "I never read such a stupid book; and look," added she, pointing to the pencil-marks on the page, "what a long hard lesson I have to learn! Miss Thompson says, that now I am seven years old, I ought to begin to learn grammar; but I do not want to learn grammar; it is all nonsense; only see what a number of hard words that I cannot understand!"

Her mother took up the book, and observed that the lesson marked out for her to learn was not the beginning of the Grammar.

"No mamma, the beginning is all about the letters of the alphabet, and spelling; but I am sure I know my letters, vowels, and consonants too, and I can spell pretty well; so Miss Thompson said I might begin here," and she pointed out the place to her mother, who read as

1

follows:—"There are in the English language nine sorts of words, or parts of speech: article, noun, pronoun, adjective, verb, adverb, preposition, conjunction, and interjection."

When she had finished, Mary said, "Well, mamma, is not all that nonsense?"

"No, my dear; but it is very difficult for you to understand, so you may skip over that. Let us see what follows." Mary seemed much pleased, and her mother continued reading. "An article is a word prefixed to nouns to point them out, and show how far their signification extends."

"Well, mamma, that is as bad as the rest; and if it is not real nonsense, it is nonsense to me at least, for I cannot understand it; so pray let us skip over that too."

"Let us see if something easier comes next," said her mother, and she went on reading. " 'A noun is the name of any thing that exists; it is therefore the name of any person, place, or thing.' Now, Mary, I think you can understand that: what is your brother's name?"

"Charles," replied Mary.

"Well then, Charles is a noun, because it is the name of a person."

"And am *I* a noun as well as Charles, mamma?"

"*I* is not your name," replied her mother; "when I call you, I do not say, 'Come here I.' "

"Oh no, you say, 'Come here, Mary.' "

"Then *Mary* is a noun, because it is your name."

"But sometimes you say, 'Come here, child;' is child a noun as well as Mary?"

"Yes, because you are called child as well as Mary."

"And when I am older, mamma, I shall be called a girl, and not a child; and is girl a noun too?"

"Yes, every name is a noun."

"Then papa is a noun, and mamma is a noun, and little Sophy is a noun, and baby is her other noun, because it is her other name; and John and George. Oh, what a number of nouns! Well, I think I shall understand nouns at last;" and her countenance began to brighten up.

"There are a great number of other nouns," said her mother. "Sheep and horses, cats and dogs, in short, the names of all animals are nouns, as just as much nouns as the names of persons."

"But the Grammar does not say so, mamma?"

"It is true," replied her mother, "that it does not mention animals; but when it says that a noun is the name of any thing that exists, animals certainly exist, so they are nouns."

"Well, I think, mamma, the Grammar ought to have said persons and animals."

"Or it might have said animals alone: for persons are animals, you know, Mary."

"Oh yes, I know that men, women, and children

are all animals; and they are nouns, as well as geese and ducks, woodcocks and turkeys: oh! and my pretty canary-bird too; and I suppose the names of ugly animals, such as rats, and frogs, and toads, and spiders, are nouns also?"

"Certainly," replied her mother; "but look, Mary, the Grammar says that the name of a place is also a noun."

"What place, mamma?"

"All places whatever. A town is the name of a place that people live in."

"Yes," said Mary; "so London, and Hampstead, and York, are nouns; but a house is a place people live in, too, mamma."

"Therefore *house* is a noun as well as *town*. What is this place we are now sitting in called, Mary?"

"It is called a room, so *room* is the name of a place to sit in, and *stable* a place to keep horses in, and *dairy* a place to keep milk and butter in; and they are all nouns." "And *cupboard* is a noun, mamma, because it is a place to keep sweetmeats in."

"Certainly," replied her mother.

"Then the *house* and the *garden*, and the *church* and the *fields*, are nouns? What great nouns!" exclaimed Mary; "and are little places nouns?"

"Certainly, this little box is a place to hold sugar plums, therefore box is a noun; and the key-hole of the door is a place to put the key in, so key-hole is a noun."

"And drawer is a noun, I am quite sure, mamma; for it is a place I keep my toys in. But, mamma, I think the key-hole of the lock, and the box for sugar plums, are more like things than places?"

"They are both; for things that are made to hold something, such as a drawer and a box, are also places; especially if they are made for the purpose of keeping the things safe."

"Oh yes," said Mary; "papa's desk is a place where he keeps his letters and bills so carefully; you know, mamma, I am never allowed to touch any thing in it. Then there is the tea-chest, which is a place and a thing too. It is a very pretty thing, and a very safe place; for you know you always keep it locked. Oh, I begin to like nouns, they make me think of so many pretty things."

"I am glad to hear it, my dear," said her mother; "but I think we have had enough of them to-day. You must not learn too much at once, or you will not be able to remember what you learn. We shall find enough to say on nouns for a second lesson."

LESSON II

CLASSES OF NOUNS

THE following day Mary came skipping into the room with her Grammar in her hand.

"Well, my dear," said her mother, "I am glad to see that your face is not quite so long as it was at the beginning of your last lesson."

"Oh no, mamma," said Mary; "it is quite a different thing now that you talk to me about my Grammar, and explain it so nicely."

"I do not promise you, Mary, that it will be always entertaining. We cannot learn without taking pains; but if you understand what is taught you, the pains are not very painful," said she, smiling.

"Well, you have now learnt that nouns are the names of persons and of places; but the Grammar says that they are also the names of things."

"Oh yes, I understand that, without any pains at all, mamma; do, pray, let me tell you what things are nouns."

"I hope you do not mean to name them all," said her

mother; "for as you know that every thing is a noun, you would never have finished."

"Oh no," replied Mary; "I cannot name every thing in the whole world, only some of those I know best. Table is a noun, and chair, and stool, and my doll, and my toys, too:—but, mamma," cried she, suddenly interrupting herself, "if every thing is a noun, what can the other parts of speech be?"

"The *name* of every thing is a noun, my dear; but not every word. The words *for* and *pretty*, for instance, are not nouns."

"No," said Mary; "for the words *for* and *pretty* are neither persons, places, nor things; so they cannot be nouns. When I want to find out a noun I must think of a person, place, or thing."

"And name it," added her mother.

"Well, but, mamma, if I were to teach Sophy grammar,—I mean, when she is a little older—do you know how I should set about it?"

"No, indeed, I cannot guess," said her mother, laughing; "but I should be very curious to know what new method you have discovered, after such a profound study of grammar as you have made."

"Nay, mamma, do not laugh at me," said Mary, half vexed.

"Well, come, tell me what your method is?"

"Why, then, I should tell Sophy that a noun is the name of every thing, and then it would be done at once;

for when she knew that every thing was a noun, there would be nothing more to learn about it."

"Your method," said her mother, "is the most simple and correct; but do you not think that if she learnt it thus all at once, she might forget it all at once, also? Do you not think that all we have said about nouns, and the dividing them into classes of persons, places, and things, has helped to imprint them on your memory?"

"So it has, mamma. I should not have remembered half so well what a noun was, if we had not talked of so many, and found out whether they were persons, places, or merely belonged to things."

"When you speak of one noun only," said her mother, "it is called singular, because it means one single thing— as a horse, or a box, or a chair; but if you speak of more than one, it is called plural."

"Yes, I know that," said Mary; "but look, mamma! there is a singular noun, called a carriage, trotting down the hill so fast!"

"Does the carriage trot, my dear?"

"Oh no, I mean the horses; but you know they are nouns too, as well as the carriage, only they are plural. Horses are nouns, because they are the names of animals; and a carriage is a noun, because it is the name of a place—or of a thing," said she, interrupting herself; "but it is certainly not the name of a person."

"But," said her mother, "there are some persons in the place, perhaps?"

8

"Yes," said Mary, "a carriage is a place that holds *people*, not *things* like a box or drawers."

"I think I have seen things in a carriage, Mary, and felt them too, very inconveniently, when we go into the country, and it is full of packages: but what is there in this carriage?"

"I cannot tell yet, mamma, it is too far off:—oh, now I see a gentleman and a lady; and they are nouns, because they are persons; but, I cannot see inside to know whether there are any parcels."

"And do you hear the sound of the carriage wheels?"

"Yes, that I do," replied she; "it makes a fine noise; the horses are trotting so fast."

"Well, then, *noise* is a noun; for whatever you can hear is a noun: and you can hear a noise."

Mary looked astonished; "Then, mamma," said she, "nouns are not only things of all kinds, but other words besides; for noise and sound are not things, at least not like common things, such as chairs and tables."

"That is true," said her mother; "they are of a different nature, but still they are things. Whatever you can hear, see, taste, smell, or feel, is a noun. Do you not say, a loud noise is a very disagreeable thing—a sweet sound is a pleasant thing? Sound and smell are therefore things; but these nouns are certainly rather more difficult for you to understand, than those which you call common nouns; but you must take pains to remember, that whatever we discern by any of our five senses is a noun."

"Our five senses!" repeated Mary: "those are seeing, hearing, smelling, tasting, and feeling."

"And by what sense do you discern those nouns which you call common, such as tables and chairs?"

"Why, we see tables and chairs, and we can touch them too if we please; so we know them by two senses, seeing and feeling."

"And we discern a sound by the sense of hearing."

"Then," said Mary, "thunder is a noun, because I can hear it; and lightning is a noun, because I can see it; and you are a noun, mamma, over and over again; for, first, you are a person, then, I can see you, and feel you when I touch you, and hear you when you speak, but I cannot smell you."

Her mother then took out her handkerchief, and Mary exclaimed, "Oh! I can smell you now so sweet!" and she jumped upon her mother's lap to smell the perfumed handkerchief.

"I hope you are not going to taste me, Mary," said her mother, drawing back, and laughing.

"But now be serious, Mary, for I am going to explain to you some nouns, which are more difficult than all the others."

Mary put on a very grave and attentive look.

"These nouns," continued her mother, "cannot be discerned by the senses, for they belong not to the body but to the mind; *virtue, honesty, happiness, greatness, goodness, wickedness*, are nouns of this description."

"Well!" exclaimed Mary, "I never should have thought these words were the names of things."

"Not of bodily things, which we can see, or feel, or perceive by any of our senses; but they are the names of things which belong to the mind, of which we can understand the meaning. If I say, *"Happiness* is the reward of a good conscience, you understand what I mean by happiness?"

"Oh yes! it is something we like very much; that every body likes; *happiness* gives us joy and pleasure, and all sorts of good things."

"And what is *goodness?"* inquired her mother.

"Goodness," replied Mary, "is doing every thing that is right; and *greatness* is something very large."

"Or *greatness,"* observed her mother, "may relate not to the body, but to the mind. Alexander was called *the Great* from his conquests, though he was but a little man."

"But," said Mary, "you say that we cannot perceive these nouns by our senses, and yet I am sure I can *feel happiness*, and *kindness*, and *goodness*, and all those difficult nouns."

"What you feel is a sensation of the mind," replied her mother; "but we cannot feel such nouns with our bodily senses as we do tables and chairs."

"Oh, no, certainly," said Mary, "it is quite a different sort of feeling."

Their attention was then caught by the carriage stopping at the door. "Oh, mamma," cried Mary, "they are getting out. It is uncle and aunt Howard. I am so glad!—and uncle and aunt are nouns,—and I hope the little nouns are come too; you know who I mean, mamma?—Emily and Mary."

"We must go and meet them," said her mother. Mary ran on first, and arrived at the door just in time to receive them,—uncle and aunt, and cousins, too. To Mary's delight, the whole family were come to spend the day, and grammar was no more thought of.

LESSON III

PRONOUNS

"Well, Mary," said her mother, the following day, "what difficult lesson of grammar have you to learn now?"

"Oh, my grammar is not half so difficult as it was, mamma," replied Mary.

"Or as you thought it was, my dear."

"Yes, but, indeed, it was very difficult till you explained it to me: now let me see what comes after nouns;" and she read,— " 'A pronoun is a word put instead of a noun, to avoid the too frequent repetition of the same word.' I do not understand that at all, mamma."

"I will tell you a story that will make you understand it." Mary's eyes brightened at the thought of a story; but her mamma told her it would consist of only a few phrases, to explain the pronoun. "There was a little boy, and the boy climbed up a tree, for the boy wanted to gather some cherries. So the boy laid hold of the branches, but the boy was so busy gathering the cherries, that the boy lost the boy's hold; so the boy fell to the ground, and the boy was very much hurt."

"What a number of boys you have said, mamma!" observed Mary, "and yet there was but one."

"And is it not tiresome," replied her mother, "to hear the same word repeated so often?"

"Yes; why do you not say the boy climbed up the tree, and he gathered cherries, and he fell down and hurt himself?"

"Then you think it better to put *he* instead of *boy*, to avoid the too frequent repetition of the noun?"

"Oh yes, now I understand it. Boy is a noun, and *he* is put instead of the boy, that is, instead of a noun, so *he* must be a pronoun; and are there a great many pronouns, mamma?"

"Not so many as there are nouns, for *he* will stand for other nouns besides a boy. Look at that man, yonder, *he* is whistling to his dog: what is the word *he* put for there, Mary?"

"Oh, *he* is put instead of man. The dog follows him, mamma; *he* is very obedient. So, then, *he* will do for boy and man, and dog too."

"Very well; I am glad to see you understand it. Now can you tell me what pronoun you would use for that little girl with a blue bonnet, whom you see walking there?"

"Oh, what a pretty blue bonnet she has, mamma!"

"Well, you have said the pronoun without thinking of it."

"Did I?" said Mary, surprised. "What was it?"

"You said, *she* has a very pretty blue bonnet."

"Ah, so I did: *she* is the pronoun put instead of the little girl; and *she* will do, also, for the lady, who is with the little girl, just as *he* stands both for the man and the boy. Do you think she is her mamma?"

"Whose mamma, my dear?"

"The little girl's mamma."

"And why did you say *her* mamma, instead of the little girl's mamma?"

"Oh, because it is much shorter and easier to say *her*, than to say little girl over and over again. Ah! now I guess why you smile, mamma: *her* must be a pronoun for the little girl as well as *she*. So, then, there is more than one pronoun for the little girl?"

"Yes, and there is more than one pronoun for man also; you may say *he* or *him*, or *his*: as *he* has a gun in *his* hand, and a dog following *him*. The pronouns, *he*, *his*, and *him*, all relate to the man."

"Then," said Mary, "if there is more than one pronoun for one noun, what a great number of pronouns there must be."

"Not so many as you think; for observe that the same pronoun will stand for a great many nouns."

"Yes," said Mary, "as *he* stands for man and boy, and dog, and *she* stands both for lady and little girl."

"You said just now, 'I am very hungry;' whom does *I* mean?"

15

"It means *me*, mamma."

"And whom does *me* mean?"

"Why, your little Mary, you know, mamma."

"Well, then, *I* and *me* are both pronouns, which you say, instead of Mary, when you speak of yourself. But little Sophy does not know yet what pronouns mean; and she says, 'Give Sophy some bread; Sophy is very hungry.' "

"Ah, so she does," said Mary, "because she has not learnt grammar."

"But *you* used pronouns before you learnt grammar, Mary."

Mary was a little puzzled to know how she could use pronouns without having learnt them. At length she said, "I knew what *I* and *me*, and *she*, and *her*, and *him* meant, though I did not know that they were pronouns, and that they were used instead of nouns."

"Well, Sophy does not even know what *I* and *me*, and *she*, and *her*, and *him* mean; so she does not use pronouns yet."

"And when will you teach her, mamma?"

"She will learn it as you did: by hearing pronouns frequently repeated, she will at last find out what they mean. Now tell me when I speak to you, what do I say instead of Mary?"

"You say dear child, sometimes."

"And do I not often say *you?* I say, 'Are *you* tired of walking? Will *you* sit down?'"

"Then is *you* my name, mamma, as well as Mary?"

"No, it is put instead of your name. A pronoun never names a person or a thing, but points them out, without naming them."

"A pronoun is a funny sort of word," said Mary, "for it talks of people, and tells you who they are, without telling you their name. Well! when I want to find out a pronoun, I shall think of some person, and find out a word that will stand for him, without mentioning his name. Now I am thinking of my writing master, and the pronoun *he* will do for him."

"Very well, Mary; but you must have mentioned the writing master's name, before you use the pronoun; otherwise I could not tell whom you meant by *he;* for he, you know, will stand for any man."

"Oh yes," said Mary; "it is only when we have been talking about the writing master that I can use the pronoun, else you would not know what *he* I meant. But, mamma, when I spoke to *you,* I did not say your name first, and you afterwards."

"No, that is not necessary; when you speak to a person, you know to whom you are talking, so that there is no occasion to mention the name. So, then, when you speak to another person, the pronoun *you* is used."

"But, when we talked about the little girl with the blue bonnet, we said *she,* not *you.*"

"Because we talked *of* her, we did not speak *to* her. If we had spoken *to* her, we might have said: '*You* have a very pretty bonnet: is that lady *your* mamma?' Now, Mary, can you find out a pronoun that will stand for both, the little girl and the lady, at the same time?"

"Oh no, mamma, that must be very difficult; for the lady is a great woman, and the little girl is quite a child: they are so different, that I cannot conceive how the same pronoun can stand for them both."

"*Them* both!" repeated her mother; "whom do you mean by *them?*"

"I mean the lady and the little girl; oh dear! *them* is the pronoun for them both; and I said it without knowing it."

"Look, Mary, *they* are just going out of sight, we can see *them* no longer;" and she laid an emphasis on *they* and *them*, to show that those two words were pronouns.

"How odd it is, mamma," said Mary, "that one pronoun should stand for two nouns at once!"

"They are plural pronouns," said her mother, "whilst those which are put in the place of one single noun are singular."

"Then *he*, and *she*, and *him*, and *her*, are singular pronouns," said Mary; "and *they*, and *them*, and *their*, are plural. Now do let me try if I can find an example." Then, after thinking a few moments, she exclaimed with exultation, as if she had made a great discovery, "Look at those sheep, mamma; *they* are feeding in the field. Here is a box of sugar plums, may I taste *them?* See, mamma, what a number of nouns I have made the pronouns stand for; all the sheep, and all the sugar plums!"

"But, the sheep and the sugar plums make only two nouns, my dear."

"What do you mean, mamma? Don't you see how many sheep there are in that field? and then the whole box is full of sugar plums?"

"All the sheep," replied her mother, "are sheep; and sheep is one noun, or one name for those animals we see feeding. Then, all the sugar plums in the box is one noun also; and in the multiplication table, I believe, Mary, that twice one make two."

Mary laughed, and her mother continued, "Now, the lady and the little girl are two different sorts of nouns."

"Yes," said Mary, "they are not just alike, as the sheep are, and the sugar plums are. But, cannot one pronoun stand for a great many different sorts of nouns?"

"Certainly; look at the nosegay I gathered this morning; there are *roses, jessamine, pinks, carnations,* and a variety of other flowers; *they* smell very sweet, and *their* colours are very bright. The pronouns I have been teaching you are called personal, because they stand for persons and things, but there are other pronouns, which I shall not explain to you at present, as they are too difficult."

Her mother then gave her a piece of cake, and told

her she might go and play in the garden, as her lesson was now over.

"Oh, mamma!" cried Mary, "I have found out a pronoun all alone; not a pronoun that stands for a great many nouns, but only for one single thing. Guess *it*, mamma;" and she laid a slight stress upon the word *it*, to help her mother.

"*It* is the word," replied her mother. Mary wondered her mamma could guess right so easily. She then ran on with a string of examples. "Here is my book, shall I put *it* by? Where is my bonnet? I must put *it* on; and my tippet? Tie *it*. So, *it* stands for every thing that is not a person or an animal."

"*It* is often used for animals also," said her mother, "especially for small ones: look at that bird, how fast *it* flies; and that caterpillar, how slow *it* crawls."

A STORY

THE BEE

A Fable from Pignotti

THE next morning, when Mary brought her Grammar, her mother said, "No, my dear, we shall not go any farther to-day, I will read you a little story, and you shall afterwards look out for all the nouns and pronouns in it. That is called parsing."

"Oh, how I shall like that!" said Mary: a story and nouns and pronouns too; how funny it will be to find them out!"

"It will require more painstaking than you are perhaps aware of; but now for the story."

"There was once a little girl——"

"Girl," said Mary, "that is a noun; and what did the little girl do?"

"She was playing alone in a pretty garden; she was very young, and ran over the beds of flowers, and rolled on the grass, filling her little hands with daisies."

"What a number of nouns and pronouns, too!" said

Mary, half to herself; "but go on, mamma, I will not interrupt you again."

"All at once," continued her mother, "the little child, as she was lying on the grass, heard a buzzing noise over her head, and looking up, she saw a large yellow and purple bee. The sun shone upon its wings, and made them look as bright as gold; and she thought it was the most beautiful insect she had ever seen. The bee whirled round and round her several times, as if at play; and every time it came nearer, she stretched out her little hand to catch it; but, it was all in vain, and at length the bee flew far away. The little girl got upon her feet as fast as she could, and ran after the bee; but, it flew about above her reach, till it was weary, and then settled to rest on a full-blown rose. When the child saw it remain quiet, she went up to the rose-bush, as gently as possible, treading softly on tiptoe; and, when she came within reach, she suddenly stretched out her hand, and grasped the bee and the rose together.

"The bee, angry at being thus disturbed, thrust out its sharp sting, and pierced through the skin of the poor little hand that held it. The wounded child screamed with pain; and the mother, hearing her cries, ran to her assistance: she took the sting out of her hand, bathed it with hartshorn, and, when the child was a little recovered from the pain and fright, her mother said:—'My dear child, do not seize hold of every thing that looks pretty, without knowing what it is; for there are many pretty things which would hurt you.'"

Mary was so much taken up with the child's

sufferings, that she quite forgot the nouns and pronouns; but when the story was ended, her mother desired her to read it over attentively, and to find out the nouns and pronouns it contained.

Mary made out above thirty nouns, and nearly as many pronouns; but she did not go through the whole story at once: her mamma divided it into parts, of six lines each; and Mary did it at different times, which made it easier for her.

LESSON IV

ADJECTIVES

THE following morning Mary came into her mamma's room with her Grammar in her hand as usual. "Well, mamma, what am I to learn to-day?" said she; "I begin to like my Grammar;" and observing her mother smile, she added, "Yes, indeed, really; and especially now that there are stories belonging to it."

"I am very glad to hear it," answered her mother: "to-day you shall learn what an *adjective* is."

"Pray explain it, mamma, for it is a very hard word."

"Let us see first what the Grammar says about it Mary;" and she read,—"An adjective is a word added to a noun, to express its quality; as a good child, a wise man."

"Oh, but mamma, I do not know what 'to express its quality' means: you must tell me all about it, or I shall never understand it."

"Quality," replied her mother, "means the sort of thing. Tell me what sort of a table is this?"

Mary, after staring at the table a few seconds, said, "It is a round table."

"Well, then, *round* is an adjective, because it points out the quality of the table."

"Oh but, mamma, it has other qualities; it is a large table: is *large* an adjective too?"

"Yes, every word added to a noun which expresses a quality, is an adjective."

"If that is all," said Mary, "an adjective is not half so difficult as I thought; I dare say that I can find out some more adjectives for the table. Let me think a little: it is a wooden table, so *wooden* must be an adjective; then it is a pretty table, and *pretty* must also be an adjective; besides, it is an *old* table, for it has been in the room, I believe, before I was born. I can't think of any more adjectives for the table," said Mary; and starting up suddenly, to look at a bird that flew across the window, she upset a flower-pot which stood upon the table. At first she was frightened, thinking she had broken it, but, finding she had but spilled the water, she said, "Oh, mamma, it's only another adjective for the table; for now," added she, "it is a *wet* table." Then, running to fetch a napkin, she wiped it carefully, and said, "And now it is a *dry* table."

"You have gained two adjectives for the table," said her mother, "and one for yourself."

"One for me, mamma? what is that?"

"Do not you think that you are an *awkward* child, to have overset the flowers?"

"Yes; but then, mamma, I am a *tidy* one, for having wiped the table *clean:* so there is another adjective for me and one for the table too. But, mamma, this other table has different adjectives; for it is *square* and *small*, not *round* and *large*, like the other."

"Very true, my dear; you see, therefore, that adjectives, by pointing out the qualities of the two tables, serve to distinguish the one from the other."

"That is," said Mary, "a round from a square table, a large from a small table, a clean from a dirty table, a wet from a dry table."

"And a tidy from an awkward girl," added her mother, laughing. "Now, Mary, can you tell me some of the adjectives belonging to that pony, which is grazing in the meadow yonder?"

"Oh, it is a pretty little pony; then it is grey; and I am sure it is spirited, it frisks about so much. Now, I believe, it is hungry, for it is eating the grass; and now, I suppose, it is tired, for it is lying down to rest. How many adjectives do you think I have said, mamma?"

"*Pretty, little, grey, spirited, hungry,* and *tired,* make no less than six."

"Why, mamma, what a great number of adjectives there must be, if there are six for the pony; and I do believe there were as many for the table. If there are six adjectives for every noun, there must be six times as many adjectives as there are nouns."

"You do not consider that the same adjectives will do for a great many different nouns; pretty, for instance."

"Oh yes, just as the same pronoun does for a great many nouns. You may say a pretty house, a pretty child, a pretty flower, a pretty bird,——"

"That is enough, Mary; you might go on for an hour, applying the adjective *pretty* to a variety of nouns."

"And it is just the same for the adjective *ugly*, is it not?"

"No, indeed; for I think there are a great many more pretty things in the world than ugly ones."

"But all adjectives will not do for all sorts of things," observed Mary; "I cannot say, a tired table, or a spirited table, or a hungry table, as I did for the pony."

"Certainly not," said her mother; "if all adjectives suited all nouns, they could not serve to distinguish the one from the other. If, when I asked you what sort of a pony was grazing in the meadow, you had told me that it had four legs, with hoofs, and a head, would that have satisfied me?"

"No, indeed; for all ponies have legs, and hoofs, and a head; so you would not know what sort of a pony it was, if I made such an answer."

"Well, then, you see that it is necessary to find out something that distinguishes one pony from another, such as being grey and pretty."

"But, mamma, there are many other ponies that are pretty and grey, besides the one in the meadow."

"That is true, but the pony we saw is one of them. The adjective does not point out qualities which distinguish one pony from all others, but qualities which distinguish some ponies from other ponies."

"But suppose," said Mary, "the pony had some quality so very strange, that no other pony in the whole world was like it. Suppose it had wings; that would distinguish it from all other ponies."

"I should then call it a monster, Mary, and not a pony; for no pony has wings."

"Cato, our black dog, must be an adjective, mamma; because black distinguishes him from dogs of another colour."

"No; there you are wrong, Mary: Cato the dog, you know, is a noun; but *black* is an adjective put before a noun, to show one of its distinguishing qualities. When you want to find out an adjective, you must think of a noun, and then observe what qualities it has."

"Well then," said Mary, "I think of my frock, which is blue; so *blue* is an adjective put before my frock to show of what colour it is; and, in the evening, *white* will be the adjective of my frock, because you know I wear a white frock in the afternoon. And are *pink* and *yellow*, and all colours, adjectives?"

"Yes; and not only colours, but every word that shows any quality of the noun: for instance, 'you are a *little* girl.' "

"Oh yes," said Mary, "little is an adjective; because it shows what sort of a girl I am; but I shall have another adjective when I am older; it will be a *great* girl."

"And I hope you may also add, a *good* girl," said

her mamma; "then, if you are attentive to your lessons, perhaps you may be distinguished by the adjective *clever.*"

"Oh, mamma," exclaimed Mary suddenly, "look at that naughty kitten! she has been playing with my two balls of scarlet and black worsted, and spoiling them."

"You have just said four adjectives," said her mother; "try if you can recollect them."

Mary thought a little, while she wound up the worsted which she had saved from the claws of the kitten, and then said, *"Naughty* kitten, *two* balls, and *black* and *scarlet* worsted. Well, mamma, I do think every thing is an adjective."

"You made the same observation upon nouns, Mary, and then you were right; for *things* are nouns; but there is not a single thing that is an adjective."

"True," said Mary; "if it is a thing it must be a noun."

"Kitten, ball, and worsted are nouns," replied her mother; "and the adjectives naughty, black, and scarlet, describe the qualities of those nouns."

"But," said Mary, "an adjective does not constantly belong to a noun; for instance, a frock may be sometimes clean, but not always."

"True," replied her mother; "but, when it is no longer clean, it is dirty, so the adjective changes from clean to dirty; and the child who wears it may be sometimes good, and at other times naughty. It is true, therefore, that the adjective or quality does not always exist in the same person or thing. You are now attentive, Mary, but the lesson has been so long, that if we do not finish it I fear you might change that adjective for one of another description."

"Ah, you mean that I should be tired and in-attentive."

"Perhaps," said her mother; "so we will put off what we have farther to say on adjectives to another day."

LESSON V

COMPARISON OF ADJECTIVES

THE next morning Mary came running into the room, holding a new box in her hand. "Look, mamma," said she, "what a *pretty* box I am going to give Sophy;" and she laid an emphasis on *pretty*, to show that she understood it was an adjective.

"It is, indeed," said her mother; "but yet I think that my work-box is *prettier.*"

"Oh, to be sure; but then the new box aunt Howard gave me is the *prettiest* of all."

"So then, Mary, one box is *pretty*, another is *prettier*, and the third is *prettiest.*"

"And are all these *pretties* adjectives, mamma? for they have not at all the same meaning."

"They have the same meaning," replied her mother, "but in different degrees. When you allow that my box is *prettier* than the box you hold, you compare the two boxes together, do you not?"

"Certainly," replied Mary; "and when I say that my new box is *prettiest*, I compare it with the other two boxes, though it is not here."

"Then you can easily understand why the adjectives *pretty, prettier,* and *prettiest,* are called degrees of comparison."

"Oh yes, because the three boxes are compared one with the other. Look at this large book, mamma," said Mary, taking up one from the table; "but there is another still larger: I can hardly lift it, it is so heavy; now I must look over all the books to find the largest, and then I shall have the three degrees of comparison. Now let me compare something that is little. Here is a little key on your bunch of keys, mamma."

"I do not think it a very small one, my dear."

"No, I did not choose a very small one; because, you know, I want to find a *littler* and a *littlest,* to show the degrees of comparison."

"But, Mary, you should not say *littler* and *littlest,* but *less* and *least.*"

"Ah! so I should," said Mary; "I thought *littler* and *littlest* did not sound right."

"In general, if you add the syllable *er* to the adjective, it gives you the first term of comparison, as tall, *taller,* small, *smaller.* And, when you add the syllable *est,* it gives you the other degree of comparison; as tall, *tallest,* small, *smallest;* but there are many exceptions to this rule."

"Yes," replied Mary, "for it did not sound right to say, little, littler, littlest, for the keys; but I might have said, small, smaller, smallest."

"Suppose I were to say, 'You are a good child, Mary;' what are the terms of comparison used for *good?*"

"Indeed I do not know; for it is not usual to say gooder and goodest, I am sure."

"No," replied her mother; "but think a little, and you will find them out."

Mary was puzzled: at last she thought of some good cake she had eaten the evening before, when she had been to play with her cousins, and then of some cake she had eaten at home, which she liked still better; and she then exclaimed, "Oh! now I have found it out,— *good* cake, *better* cake, and *best* cake,—those are the three degrees of comparison. And, mamma," added she, "I dare say you will find that I shall be a good girl, a better girl, and a best girl at last."

"I shall be very glad if I do," said her mother, smiling; "but tell me, did you eat much of this good cake with your cousins?"

"I believe I did, mamma; but Charles ate more."

"Oh! I am afraid Charles was a greedy boy," said her mother.

"No, it was Harry who was the greedy boy; for he ate the most of all. Ah! those are the three degrees of comparison,—*much, more, most*. I ate *much* cake, Charles *more*, and Harry *most*."

"The degrees of comparison, in adjectives of more than two syllables," said her mother, "are usually formed by the addition of the words *more* and *most*; for it would be tiresome to lengthen out words that have already three or four syllables: thus, if you say an agreeable woman, it is awkward to say an agreeabl*er* woman, or the agreeabl*est* woman."

"Yes, indeed," replied Mary, laughing, "that would sound very disagreeable; but you may say a *more agreeable* woman, and the *most agreeable* woman; and you may say a sensible man, a *more sensible* man, and a *most sensible* man."

"Now," said her mother, "I will tell you the names of these degrees of comparison. The first is called *Positive*. If I say this fire is hot, I mean that it is positively hot; but if I say the fire in the dining-room is hotter, then I compare the fire in the drawing-room with the fire in the dining-room; and, therefore, this degree of comparison is called *Comparative;* but where shall we find the hottest fire in the house, Mary?"

"Oh! in the kitchen, mamma, where the cook roasts the meat and dresses all the dinner."

"Well, then, the kitchen fire is hottest; and hottest is called the *Superlative* degree, which means that it is above the others."

"But, mamma, when you said, 'This fire is hot,' you did not compare it with any other fire; so how can *hot* be a degree of comparison?"

"What you observe is very true, Mary; correctly speaking, the positive adjective is not a degree of comparison."

"I will now write down a few of these terms of comparison;" and she wrote as follows:—

Positive	Comparative	Superlative
Rich	Richer	Richest
Wise	Wiser	Wisest
Large	Larger	Largest
Nice	Nicer	Nicest
Cold	Colder	Coldest

"And pray, mamma," said Mary, "write down some of the adjectives that you cannot put *er* and *est* to; you know what I mean."

"You mean," replied her mother, "when it is necessary, the word is changed, in order to express the degrees of comparison." Then she wrote:—

Positive	Comparative	Superlative
Good	Better	Best
Bad	Worse	Worst
Little	Less	Least
Much	More	Most

"Adjectives," continued Mrs. B., "have no number; they are neither singular nor plural: you say 'a good man,' and 'good men;' a 'little child,' and 'little children.'"

"But why should they not have number as well as

pronouns?" asked Mary; "I think we ought to make them singular and plural, and say *sweets oranges*, not sweet oranges."

"If you said sweets instead of sweet, it would only show you that the noun oranges was plural, and you knew that before, therefore it would be telling you the same thing twice over."

"Then I suppose," said Mary, "that adjectives have no person either?"

"No," replied her mother; "in the English language adjectives have neither person, number, nor gender; for the nouns to which they belong tell you both their person, number, and gender; and being told a thing once is as good as a hundred times—that is, provided you take care to remember it."

"But," said Mary, "there is one thing about adjectives I cannot understand. If you say a silk gown, silk is a noun and yet it is used as an adjective, for it shows the quality of the gown."

"Nouns are often used as adjectives," replied her mother: "Thus silver, when spoken of as a metal, is a noun, but if added to teapot, it becomes an adjective; you think of it only as the quality of the teapot."

"Then," said Mary, "copper, when spoken of as a metal, is a noun, but if it is added to saucepan or coal-scuttle, it becomes an adjective, because it shows the quality of the saucepan or the coal-scuttle. Then *leather* shoes, *cotton* stockings, *brass* buttons, *cloth* coats, are all adjectives added to the nouns shoes, stockings, buttons, coats."

"Or, at least," observed her mother, "they are used as adjectives: and here we will conclude the lesson."

LESSON VI

ARTICLES

AT the next lesson of grammar, Mary's mother told her there were only two more words to be learnt which relate to nouns, and these were the articles *an* or *a* and *the*.

"They are the parts of speech which the grammar begins with," said Mary: "here they are," added she, opening the book and reading. " 'An article is a word prefixed to nouns to point them out and show how far their signification extends, as *an* orange, *a* man, *a* house, *the* dog.' "

"And you may recollect, Mary, that you begged to skip over the articles, to which I consented, as I thought them too difficult for you to begin with; but, now that you have learnt three of the other parts of speech, you will easily understand what an article means."

"I will try, mamma, if you will explain it."

"Let us first consider the sense or meaning of the articles, and the difference between *a* and *the*. Suppose the gardener were to come in and say, 'An oak has been blown down in the garden;' I should not know which of the oaks had been blown down."

"Oh, mamma!" cried Mary, eagerly, "I know what you would do; you would ask the gardener about its adjectives, to know whether it was a large or a small oak, or young or old, or pretty or ugly."

"But that would not quite satisfy me," said her mother; "I should want to know, not only what sort of an oak it was that was blown down, but which particular oak it was; and adjectives will not always tell me that."

Mary was disappointed that she had not guessed right, and she said, "Then, mamma, you need only ask him which oak it was, and he might reply, '*The* great tree that grew on the bank.'"

"So you see," said her mother, "*the* points out that one particular oak has been blown down; whilst *a* only means that it is some oak or other, without saying which."

"But, mamma, *the* would not show you which oak was blown down, until the gardener told you that it was the great oak that stood on the bank."

"That is true, my dear; *the* does not tell you which oak it is, but it tells you that the explanation is coming; for, whenever the article *the* is used to distinguish one thing from others, some description is sure to follow, or has been given before: the sense is not complete without it; and, if the gardener only said, *the* oak, I should not understand him; but when he adds, *which stood on the bank*, the meaning is clear; or, if there had been more than one oak on the bank, he might have said, 'The great oak which stood on the bank.' If I asked the gardener whether any building had been blown down, and he answered, yes, *the* church steeple, *the* would not require any further explanation."

"No," replied Mary, "for as there is only one steeple, you need not inquire which. I understand it now very well, it is only when there are several things to distinguish that *the* requires some explanation."

"And do you understand the difference between *a* and *the?*"

"I think so," said Mary; "suppose I were to say, 'Pray, mamma, give me *an* apple,' I should mean any apple you liked; but, if you took me to the apple-shop, I dare say that I should ask leave to choose it, and I should say, 'Pray give me the apple with the pretty red and yellow streaks.' "

"Very well," said her mother, "*the* would point out that you wished to have one particular apple, and *pretty red and yellow streaks* would show me which it was."

"Oh, yes!" said Mary, "the *pretty red and yellow streaks* are the adjectives—I mean *pretty, red,* and *yellow,* for I know *streaks* is a noun; and these adjectives help to distinguish the apple from the others; so, you see, mamma, the article *the* would not do alone to show which apple I wished for."

"No," replied her mother; "the article *the* only points out that a particular description of the apple will immediately follow. In the description, adjectives, nouns, and all sorts of words, may be used, in order to show exactly which one is meant."

LESSON VII

INDEFINITE ARTICLES

"THE article *an*," said Mary's mother, "can be used before nouns of the singular number only; you cannot say, *an* apples, *an* eggs."

"Oh, no," said Mary, laughing; "but you may say, *the* apple as well as *the* apples, and *the* egg as well as *the* eggs; so *the* is both singular and plural."

"Yes," said her mother, "*the* can be used before nouns, whether singular or plural; whilst *an* can be used only before a noun singular, and the reason of that is, because *an* only means 'one,' and was at first the same word; until, in speaking quickly, it became altered. *The* is called the definite article, because it defines or points out the particular object which is afterwards described, as in the instance, 'The great oak that grew on the bank.' *A* is called the indefinite article, because it does not define any thing, or point out any particular object."

"Mamma, will you give me *an* doll?" said Mary; "that is the indefinite article."

"But do you think that sounds right, Mary?"

"No, I think I ought to say, 'Give me *a* doll;' but is *a* an article? *A* is not a word; it is only a single letter."

"That is no reason why it should not sometimes make a word of itself; the pronoun *I* is only a single letter, but that letter makes an entire word."

"True," said Mary; "I never observed that *I* was only one letter; I suppose, because it is a great letter, and so it looks more like a word by itself."

"*I* is always written with a capital letter; but, my dear, it is the sense, and not the size or the sort of letter that you must think of. The article *a* is a capital letter when it begins a sentence, as 'A man came here;' but it is a small letter if it comes in the middle of a sentence, as, 'Give me *a* shilling.'"

"When the noun begins with a consonant, as doll does, the article *an* is changed into *a*, merely on account of the sound; for the meaning is the same. You know which of the letters are called consonants?"

"Oh, yes, a, e, i, o, u, and y, are vowels; and all the others are consonants."

"Well, then, think of some noun that does not begin with a vowel, and see whether you must not change the article *an* into *a* before it."

Mary thought a little, and then said, "Cat begins with a consonant; so I must say *a* cat, not *an* cat."

"And you must, for the same reason, say, a dog, a ship, a book; and, as most of the nouns begin with a consonant, the indefinite article is more commonly used in this form than in the other; for, as I told you before, people, who wished to speak quickly, found it much easier to say, 'a dog, a ship,' than 'one dog,' 'one ship.' You may try, if you like, whether it is easier to say, one man sat on one bank in one field, with one dog by him; he had one apple in his hand, one stick on his shoulder, with one bundle at the end of it; or, a man sat on a bank in a field, with a dog by him; he had an apple in his hand, a stick on his shoulder, with a bundle at the end of it."

"But there is one consonant in which *a* need not be used instead of *an;* it is when the noun begins with an *h* which is not aspirated: you know what aspirating the *h* is?"

"Oh, yes!" replied Mary; "I know I must draw a long breath to aspirate the *h*," and she repeated, horse, hand, heart. "You always make me aspirate the *h*'s when I read, mamma."

"Not always; for they should not always be aspirated. In the word hour the *h* is not aspirated, but it is in the words horse and hat; therefore, although you say an hour, you say, a horse, a hat; not an horse, an hat."

"Oh, no!" said Mary; "that would sound very ill."

"*The*," continued her mother, "never changes, because *the* hour sounds as well as *the* horse, though in hour the *h* is not aspirated, and in horse it is."

"Then, mamma, after all, there are three articles instead of two—an, a, and the?"

"No," replied her mother; "*a* and *an* have exactly the same meaning, and are therefore called the same article. *An* comes from an old Saxon word, *ein*, which means *one;* and *a* is nothing but *an* with the *n* left out before a consonant."

"Then," said Mary, "I think the indefinite article should be called *an* instead of *a*."

"They have both an equal right to that title," replied her mother; "but as there are a great many more words which begin with consonants than with vowels, *a* is usually called the indefinite article, and *n* is added to it when the following word begins with a vowel. In many languages the indefinite article and the word *one* are the same; in French it is *un*, as *un homme*, which means both *a man* and *one* man."

"Oh, then," said Mary, "that was the reason why the French lady who came here the other day called me *one* little girl. It seemed to me very strange, because she could not doubt whether I was *one* or *two* little girls; but now I understand it: she only meant to say that I was *a* little girl."

"Yes," replied her mother, "she supposed that in English, as in French, the number *one* and the indefinite article *a* were the same thing."

"And why are they not so?" asked Mary.

"Because it is much quicker and easier to say *a* than *one;* to say a man, a dog, a ship, than one man, one dog, one ship."

"Can *a* and *the* be put before pronouns as well as nouns?" inquired Mary.

"No, my dear; you cannot say *a* he, *the* she, *an* it: that would be quite nonsense."

"Articles," continued her mother, "can be placed only before a noun, or before an adjective which is followed by a noun. A pretty, a hard, the high, the blue, is nonsense. Sometimes, indeed, an article is put before an adjective without a noun, when we know pretty well what noun is meant, by what we are talking of. So, in speaking of ships, it is not unusual to say, they go down to the deep, meaning, 'the deep sea;' and, in speaking of men, it is not unusual to say, the rich, the poor, the proud, the brave; meaning, the rich men, the poor men, the proud men, the brave men, and so on. But this can only be done when there is not much doubt of the noun which is meant. But, a pretty flower, a hard stone, the high hill, the blue sky, is sense of itself; you can understand the meaning of each of those phrases clearly."

"Oh, yes! they are very short," said Mary; "only three words in each, an article, an adjective, and a noun, and those three words make sense. Then, mamma, if I wanted to know whether a word were a noun or not, I have only to put an article before it, and see whether it makes sense or nonsense. If I put *a* before *tall*, I know that tall is not a noun, because, *a tall* is nonsense; but if I put *a* before *man* or *house*, I know that man and house are nouns, because *a man*, or *a house*, is sense."

"That is very true, Mary; but I think it is a still better method to know whether a word is a noun or not by understanding its meaning. We may now take leave of articles, and end our lesson for to-day."

"But, mamma, you will tell me a little story, will you not, that I may find out the articles in it? That will help me to remember them."

"Very well," replied her mother, "I will read you the story now, for you have had quite enough grammar to-day; but then to-morrow you must find out, not only the articles in it, but the nouns, pronouns, and adjectives also."

A STORY

THE HEN AND CHICKENS

A HEN, who was confined under a hencoop in a poultry yard, had a large brood of young chickens; I believe there were no fewer than twelve of them; they were so small that they could get in and out of the coop between the twigs of the wicker-work, but the hen was too large to get out; and she was sadly afraid of her little chickens running away and being lost. So, when they went out of the coop, she called after them, as you have heard hens call their chickens, cluck! cluck! cluck! and, when the chickens heard her, they ran back into the coop. She sometimes picked up grains of corn to give them to eat; and sometimes she gathered them under her wings, and kept them as warm and snug as if they had been in a nice bed.

One day the hen saw a large hawk flying high up in the air. She knew that it was a bird of prey, that is, a bird which seizes on small birds, and carries them away. The hen was terribly frightened, lest the hawk should pounce down upon one of her little chickens, seize it in his sharp talons, and carry it away; so she kept calling out cluck! cluck! cluck! as loud as she could, and the chickens came running into the coop, one after the other, as fast as their little legs could carry them. They all got safe in and hid themselves under her wings, except one little chicken, which had strayed so far from the coop that it could not hear the hen call. It had been playing about with some ducklings, and, when the mother duck called her young ones, the little chicken went with them to see what they were going to do. The great duck was not kept under a coop like the hen, but she waddled about wherever she chose, and the little ducklings followed her. She led them to a pretty little round pond in the poultry yard; and, when she got to the edge of the water, she stepped in and began to swim; then the little ones all followed her into the pond, and the poor chicken was quite frightened, for she thought they would be drowned; but, to her great surprise, they began paddling about in the water with their webbed feet, and could swim almost as well as their mother. Then the little chicken thought that it must be very easy to swim, and it looked as if it was very pleasant, so she resolved to follow her little playfellows, and into the pond she went. She tried to move her legs as she saw the ducklings do; but it was all in vain: she could not swim; and when she found herself sinking in the water she fluttered her wings, but that would not do either; she could not fly: she then struggled to reach the edge of the pond; but her feet no longer felt the ground and she was very near being drowned.

Helen, a little girl who lived at the farmhouse to which the poultry belonged, took great pleasure in going every morning after breakfast to feed the poultry with the crumbs of bread she gathered from the breakfast-table. She went first to the hencoop, to see the brood of young chickens, who were just then her favourites; and, seeing the hen appear much ruffled, and the chickens crouched closely under her wings, she asked Betty, the dairy-maid, what was the matter.

"Oh, Miss Helen!" said Betty, "there has been a hawk flying over the poultry yard, which has frightened all the poor creatures; but, what is the worst of all, I fear that it has carried off one of the little chickens, for I have just been counting them over to see if they were all safe, and I can find only eleven." The tears rushed into poor Helen's eyes; but her mamma, who was with her, said, "Let us search every where, to see whether we cannot find it, Helen; that will be much better than crying." So they hunted all through the henhouse, and under some fagots of wood, and a litter of straw, in short, all over the poultry yard, till at last they came to the pond. "It is of no use to look there," said Helen, "for the chicken cannot swim." However, as her mamma went on, Helen followed; and, when they were close to the water's edge, what should they see, but the poor little chicken, whose strength was almost exhausted, still faintly struggling to get out. "Oh! there it is, indeed, mamma," cried Helen, gasping for breath, between delight and fear. Her mother seized a wooden shovel, which happened to lie on the ground, and, pushing it into the water under the chicken, brought it safely ashore. Helen hugged it in her arms, though it was wringing with wet, and carried it into the house, where she dried its feathers, warmed it well, and then gave it some crumbs of bread to eat. "I need not give it any water, mamma," said she; "I am sure it has had enough of that, and I dare say the mere sight of water would frighten it; but I believe the crumbs frighten it too, for see, mamma, it will not eat."

"The best comfort you can give the poor bird, Helen," said her mother, "is to take it back to the coop; it will recover more quickly under its mother's wing than any where else." Helen longed to nurse the chicken a little longer; but, when she found she could not make it eat, she carried it back to the poultry yard and put it under the coop.

"The hen was quite happy to see it safe back. She stretched out her wings for it to nestle under them: then she picked up some grains of corn, which she gave it to eat; and the poor chicken was so glad to get back to its mother, after all the fright it had had, that it thought it would never leave her any more.

"Now, Mary," said her mother, "this story is a great deal too long for you to find out the nouns, pronouns, and adjectives it contains in one day. I advise you to divide it into portions of six or eight lines, and make each of them a separate lesson of parsing."

LESSON VIII

VERBS

THERE had been no lesson of grammar during a whole week, in order that Mary might have time to fix in her memory what she had already learned, before she began any thing new. At length she brought her exercise, and showed her mother that she had gone through the whole of the story of the Hen and Chickens, and had found out in it the several parts of speech she had learned. Her mother then thought it time to go on to the Verbs. Mary accordingly fetched her grammar, and her mother read as follows:—

"A verb is a word which signifies to be, to do, or to suffer."

"I cannot understand that at all," said Mary, looking very grave.

"You will like the verbs that do something best," said her mother, "so we will begin with them. Come here, Mary;" and, as Mary approached, she added, "Well, what are you doing now?"

"I mean to come to you, mamma, as you desired me."

"Then *come* is a verb; and how do you come?"

"You see, mamma," said Mary, smiling—"I *walk*; and is *walk* a verb too?"

"Yes, certainly."

Mary then began to run. "Now I am doing another verb," said she; "*run* must be a verb also," and presently she ran out of the room. Her mother wondered what she was gone for: but she soon came back with her skipping-rope; and skipped very lightly round the room, looking all the while at her mamma, and smiling, as much as to say, "You see I know that *skip* is a verb too." When she reached the door, off she went again, but soon returned with her hoop, which she trundled round the table.

"Very well, Mary; I see that you understand that to skip and to trundle are verbs; but, if you run away every time you find out a new verb, we shall not get on much; so now sit down on that chair." Mary seated herself, and her mother asked her what she was doing then.

"Nothing at all, mamma; I am sure I cannot be doing a verb now, for I sit quite still.

"But there are some still quiet verbs, Mary, as well as busy ones. When you sit down you do something, for you sit; besides you were speaking to me, and to speak is a verb also."

Mary began laughing. "Oh, what a number of verbs there are!" said she.

"To laugh is another verb," said her mother, "and sometimes a very noisy one."

"So, then, you may do a verb," said Mary, "without moving about, if to sit, and to speak, and to laugh, are verbs?"

"Yes; and you may *do* a verb (as you call it) even without the slightest motion of any part of your body; for the actions of the mind are verbs as well as those of the body; so, to *think*, to *hope*, to *fear*, to *wish*, are verbs, as well as to *ride*, to *walk*, to *eat*, and to *drink*."

"While I was working this morning, mamma, I was wishing that my cousins might come to-day, and hoping that they would, and thinking all about it; but it seemed to me that I did not *do* any thing but work."

"Your body did nothing else, but your mind was active as you describe, and wished, and hoped, and thought; and your thoughts are a part of your mind. Now, Mary, let me hear all you have been doing this morning?"

"Oh! a great many things," replied Mary, "First, I got up; then I was washed; then I was dressed; after that I said my prayers; then I ran out into the garden; then I ate my breakfast; and, last of all, I came to you, mamma, to learn my lesson of grammar."

"What a number of things you have done, Mary; and every one of them is a verb."

"Oh! but, mamma, you know I am not old enough to wash and dress myself, so it was not I who did those two verbs, but nurse who did them for me."

"Verbs," observed her mother, "not only express the actions of the mind and of the body, but their state or manner of being; such as *being* hot or cold, or *being* hungry or tired, or *being* pleased or vexed, or *being* washed and dressed."

"Well, I am sure I am always either *being* a verb or *doing* a verb; for I am always busy about something, unless I am tired or sleepy, and those you know are *being* verbs."

"Then, Mary, verbs do not only express the action or being of men, women, and children, but of all animals and all things; as the *sky* is bright, the *flowers* are faded, the *nut* is cracked, your *frock* is torn."

"Indeed, mamma!" said Mary, looking anxiously at her frock; "I did not know it; where is it?"

"The rent will be soon mended," said her mother, smiling; "it was only a make-believe example of the state of your frock."

"Oh, mamma! there is one verb I want very much," said Mary; "I am so hungry."

"To be hungry is a verb, it is true," replied her mother; "but to want to be hungry is not very pleasant, in my opinion."

"Oh no, mamma! the verb I want is to eat."

"I rather think you would like a noun to eat," said her mother, giving her a slice of cake.

Mary began eating, and, between the mouthfuls, she said, "Now I have got the noun, and I am doing the verb." Having finished, she complained that the cake had made her thirsty. "That is one of the still quiet verbs," said she; "but I should like to do one of the more busy verbs, with a noun, mamma; can you guess what I mean?"

"I think I can; you want to drink some water."

"Indeed! how cleverly you have guessed it; to drink was the verb, and water the noun."

"I must now tell you, Mary," said her mother, "that there are three different sorts of verbs, called *active*, *passive*, and *neuter*."

"I know what an active verb means," cried Mary; "it is a busy verb, when you are doing something active, like that bird yonder. Look, mamma, how fast it flies! I am sure to fly must be an active verb."

"No, my dear," replied her mother, "it is not. An active verb means not only that you do something, but that you do it to somebody or to something else. When I say *I love*, I mean that I love somebody or something else; do I not?"

"Yes, mamma; you love me."

"But, when the bird flies, his flying has nothing to do with any one else."

"Yet, mamma, you sit quite still while you love me: how can that be an active verb?"

"I think, when I love you, Mary; so my thoughts are active, though I do not move. However, if you wish for something more active, come here;" and she gave Mary a kiss. "To kiss is an active verb, because you must kiss some person or thing. Now, Mary, if you are not satisfied," added she, laughing, "I can strike you, and you will think that active enough;" and she gave Mary several little taps.

"Oh, yes! I understand it, mamma; though the bird moved so fast, when it flew along, it did not meddle with any body or any thing in flying: so, to fly is not an active verb."

"Now, can you tell me," said her mother, "when Willy flies his kite, is it a verb active or not?"

Mary was puzzled; she thought a little, and then suddenly exclaimed, "Oh! a verb active to be sure, because he does not himself fly, like the bird, but he flies his kite, and that, you know, is making something else fly; so to fly, used in the sense of flying a kite, must be an active verb, though to fly, used in the sense of flying, one's self, like a bird, is not."

Her mother said she was right. She then added, "The person who acts is called the *agent*, and the person or thing acted upon is called the *object*. If I say, 'The horse eats corn,' can you tell me which is the agent, and which the object?"

"Yes, certainly," said Mary; "the horse is the agent, and corn the object. And when Willy flies his kite, Willy is the agent, and the kite the object. But I do not quite understand what agent means?"

"Agent means a person who acts; but perhaps you do not quite understand what acts means?"

"I think I do pretty well," said Mary: "it does not

mean a person who acts in a play, but a person who does something really."

"To act always means to do something," replied her mother, "whether it be in real life or at the theatre; agent, therefore, is the person who does something."

"Then what does papa's agent in the country mean?"

"It means a person who acts for papa in the country— that is, settles his farming business for him."

Her mother then said that she had learnt enough of verbs for one lesson, and that they would go on with them at the next.

LESSON IX

PASSIVE VERBS

WHEN Mary came with her grammar the following morning, her mother told her that the next sort of verb was called a *passive* verb, "which means," said she, "that, instead of doing any thing yourself, something is done to you. Instead of being the agent, you are the object of the verb. If you say, 'I am beaten,' it means that some one beats you, while you remain passive."

"Indeed, mamma," cried Mary, "I should not remain passive if I were beaten; I should run away as fast as I could;"—and off she ran, so close to the fire, that her mother called out, "Take care, Mary; if you go so near the fire you will be burnt. Can you tell me, what sort of a verb '*to be burnt*' is?"

"That would be something done to me, mamma; for I am sure I should not do it myself, it hurts so. It would be some*thing* not some*body* that burnt me; for it would be the fire that burnt me; but, I suppose, whether it is a thing or a person does not signify."

"No," said her mother; "it makes no difference what it is that acts upon you; to be burnt, to be beaten, to be scolded, are all passive verbs."

"Then being washed and dressed are passive verbs," said Mary. "I think passive verbs are very disagreeable; I have nothing to do but to remain quiet, and suffer something to be done to me."

"No," said her mother, "that is not necessary: if you were burnt, you would, probably, scream out for help, and run away; but, unless you extinguished the flames, so long as *you were burnt* by them, that verb would be passive. When you are acted upon, you are considered as passive, whether you remain quiet or not. *To be caught* is a passive verb, whether you struggle to get free or not: *to be thrown down* is a passive verb, though you are certainly in motion whilst falling; but you are put in motion by some person or thing acting upon you, and making you fall."

"O, yes!" said Mary; "but, if I throw myself down, it is an active, not a passive, verb."

"Yes, because you are, in that case, both the person who acts and the object acted upon. But all passive verbs, Mary, are not disagreeable; what do you think of the verb to be loved?"

"O! that is very pleasant; but, mamma, I thought you said the verb *to love* was an active verb."

"*To love* is an active verb," replied her mother, "because you love another person, and, therefore, act upon another person; but *to be loved* is when another person acts upon you: you may say, 'I am loved by Sophy.'"

"Well, then, I should love Sophy in return."

"In that case," said her mother, "you would return the active verb *to love*. In the passive verb you cannot act, nor even move, unless you are moved like a log, or some other inanimate being, as when you are thrown down; or you may be pulled, or pushed, or driven, or drawn; but, the instant you move of your own accord, the verb is no longer passive. *To be admired, to be praised, to be caressed*, are also agreeable passive verbs."

"Yet I like the active verbs the best, mamma. I had rather be the agent, and have something to do, than the object, and have something done to me."

"Then," said her mother, "you will like the third kind of verb, which is called the *neuter* verb; for there you not only do something yourself, but you do it by yourself, without acting on any thing else."

"What, like the bird that flew, mamma?"

"Exactly; *to fly* is a neuter verb, and so is *to walk* and *to run*."

"Let me think of some neuter verbs, mamma. To cough, to sneeze, to sit, to stand, to sleep, must all be neuter verbs; for when I do those verbs I do not meddle with any body or any thing else."

"True," said her mother; "but now, Mary, we have been talking so long about verbs that I think we must go into the garden to refresh ourselves! so run and put on your bonnet."

Mary was soon ready, and they went out. "Look at that snail, mamma," said she, "how slowly it crawls;—to crawl is a neuter verb, I remember that; but I will make it go a little faster:" she gathered a twig, and touched the snail with it. The snail drew in its horns.

"Oh! poor little snail," said her mother, "do not hurt it."

"Indeed, I do not hurt it, mamma, it is only frightened. *To be frightened* is a passive verb, for the snail is passive while I frighten it; but," added she, "if I say I frighten the snail, that must be an active verb."

"True, because you act upon the snail. *To frighten* is an active verb, because you must frighten some one; but *to be frightened* is a passive verb, because the frightened creature is passive."

"Yes, but, mamma, the snail, when it was frightened, drew in its horns."

"Then it became active, for *to draw in its horns* is an active verb."

"Then, mamma, the snail is both active and passive at the same time; for I am sure it is frightened when it draws in its horns."

"It is active," replied her mother, "in the verb to draw in its horns, and passive in the verb to be frightened."

Mary's attention was soon after called off by the sight of a man beating a dog.

"Oh, mamma!" exclaimed she, "look at that naughty man. I am sure *to beat* is an active verb; see how his arm moves, and what blows he gives the poor dog, who stands quite passive."

"But remember, Mary, that it is not the motion of

his arms, but his beating the dog, which makes it an active verb; for if the man, instead of beating the dog, was swimming, he would still use his arms and his legs too, and yet he would not do an active verb, because he has no object to act upon."

"Very true," replied Mary. "I wish, mamma," continued she, "that when we go in you would write down some active, and some passive, and some neuter verbs, as you did the degrees of comparison of the adjectives:" and, when they returned to the house, her mother took a pen and wrote as follows:—

Active	Passive	Neuter
To love	To be loved	To dance
To hate	To be hated	To rise
To lay	To be laid	To lie
To send	To be sent	To sit
To tease	To be teased	To stir
To bid	To be bidden	To run
To tell	To be told	To leap

"Why, mamma!" cried Mary, "the active and the passive verbs, in this list, are all the same! I do not mean the same sort of verbs, but the same words."

"That is always the case," said her mother; "reflect a little, and you will find it must be so. The active verb means that there is an agent acting upon an object; and the passive verb means that there is an object acted on by an agent; so you see that the two verbs are very closely connected."

"It seems to me, mamma, to be much the same thing."

"O, no! nothing can be more different than to act upon another, or to be acted upon by another; to beat, or to be beaten; to love, or to be loved. If you say, I love Sophy, or strawberries, or pictures, the verb is active, and Sophy, strawberries, and pictures, are the objects acted upon. But, if Sophy were to repeat the verb, what would she say?"

"She being the object loved would say, 'I am loved.'"

"The verb would then be passive; so you see that a verb active has always a corresponding verb passive."

"But, mamma," said Mary, "a strawberry, though it is an object, could not make a passive verb: for it could not say, 'I am eaten:' nor could a picture say, 'I am admired.'"

"True," said her mother; "but we might say for them, the strawberry is eaten, or the picture is admired."

"Yes," said Mary, "if I eat an apple I am the agent, that is the person who eats, and the apple is the object, that is the thing eaten. And is there an agent and an object in a passive verb, mamma?"

"Try to find out yourself, Mary: are there two persons concerned in a passive verb? In the verb to be beaten, for instance?"

"O! to be sure there are," replied Mary: "there must be one person to beat, and the other to be beaten, and the person who beats is the agent, and the person or animal beaten (for perhaps it may be a dog, you know, mamma) is the object. "But it is better to be loved than to be beaten," continued she, looking affectionately at her mamma; "if I am loved, and it is you who love me, you are the agent, and I am the object. But, then, in the neuter verb," continued Mary, "there are not two persons concerned; for the agent does the verb all alone, without meddling with any one or any thing else, so there can be no object."

"Certainly," replied her mother, "if you laugh or cry, or walk or sleep, there is no object. Try to remember these distinctions between the verb active and the verb passive, and the agent and the object: it will be very useful to you hereafter. There is a great deal more to be learnt about verbs, my dear; but I think you have had enough of them for the present."

"O! but the little story at the end, mamma, you will not forget that. Now I shall have five sorts of words to look out for—nouns, pronouns, adjectives, articles, and verbs."

"Very well, Mary, I will write you a story for to-morrow."

A STORY

THE FISHERMAN

A FISHERMAN and his wife, who were very poor, lived in a little hut by the side of a river. They had two children—Jack, a stout lad, eleven years old, and Jenny, who was only eight. The fisherman had a boat, in which he and his son used to go on the river to lay their nets: when they caught plenty of fish they were very glad, because they took them to the next market town and sold them. For several days the fisherman had caught but very few fish; and when he had but few fish to sell he could get but little money to buy food. For a long time the family had had nothing but bread and potatoes for dinner, and the poor children longed for a little meat, and some milk with their bread at breakfast. One day the fisherman, in drawing up his nets, felt that they were heavy. "Well, we have caught a fish or two at last," said he. "Come, Jack, lend me a hand to heave in the nets." This was soon done, when, to the surprise of both father and son, only three fish were found in them: one of them, it is true, was very large, but it was still more remarkable for its weight. "Why, one would think this fish was made of lead," said the fisherman: "there must be something inside."

When the fish was dead he ripped it open; and what should he find, instead of lead, but an old purse full of gold! "Well, good luck is come at last!" cried the fisherman; "this money is just in time to pay my quarter's rent; but here's enough to last for years; and I promise you a new suit of clothes, Jack."

"And there's enough to buy a new gown for Jenny, too, father, is there not?"

"Ay, and for your mother and all." They hastened home with the newly-found treasure, and the wife was no less pleased than they were; but she could not help saying, "What a sad thing it must be to the poor man who lost it!"—"Poor man!" repeated her husband; "I think he must be a rich one to have so much gold."

"Ay, while he had it," replied she; "but now that he has lost it he must be poor."

"Mayhap, he may have a deal more," said the fisherman; "however there's no finding out whom it belonged to once, so now it belongs to me, who have fished it up."

"I wonder how it got into the river," cried Jack.

"And how the fish came to swallow it," said Jenny, "for gold is not good to eat."

"No, but it will buy many things that are," replied her father; "and I promise you a rare dinner to-morrow: what do you say to a beefsteak pudding, and a pot of ale?"

They counted over twenty guineas; the fisherman's wife rubbed them as bright as she could, and put them into her husband's leathern purse; and she gave the old purse, which was quite worn out, to Jenny. There were two metal rings or runners to this purse: and little Jenny tried to rub them bright, as her mother had done the guineas. When the dirt and rust were rubbed off, she saw that there were letters engraved on the runners, and she took them to her brother, who could read a little. He examined the letters a long time, and at last made out these words:—"Mr. Cullen, Heath Lodge."

"Good heavens!" exclaimed the mother; "this purse belongs to Mr. Cullen, and we must restore it," added she, with a heavy sigh.

"But father found it," said Jack; "and if he had not fished it up, Mr. Cullen could never have had it."

"That don't signify," replied his mother; "whatever is found must be restored to the owner, if you can find out who he is."

The fisherman agreed with his wife. They regretted very much all the good things they had intended to buy with the gold; but it was settled that, the next morning while the fisherman went to draw his nets, Jack and Jenny should carry the gold to Heath Lodge, which was about two miles off, so it was put back again into Mr. Cullen's purse. The next morning away they trudged; and as they went, they talked of the number of things they could have bought with so much gold.

"If father had but kept one of the guineas, it would have bought us new clothes, and one good dinner at least," said Jenny; "and I think that would have been but fair, as he found the purse."

"Father knows best," replied Jack, "and he said that it would not be honest to keep back a single penny; but that, perhaps, the gentleman would make us a present for taking back the money."

"Oh, I dare say he will," cried Jenny: "what do you think he will give us?"

"Indeed, I can't tell," said the lad; "but mind you don't ask for any thing. Look, yonder's the house; now take care to behave yourself, Jenny, and make a low courtesy as soon as you see the gentleman."

When they were shown into Mr. Cullen's room, Jenny dropped one of her best courtesies. Jack took off his hat, scraped his foot, and then holding out the purse—"There's your purse, sir," said he; "father found it inside of a fish." Mr. Cullen was astonished at the sight of his purse.—"It is no less than two years," said he, "since I lost it. It dropped into the river one day, when I was rowing, and I never expected to see it again. The purse is spoiled, it is true, but there is every guinea in it safe."

"The runners are not spoiled," said Jenny, "for I rubbed them bright, and so Jack read your name."

"You are very good children," said Mr. Cullen, "and I thank you for restoring my purse." Jack made his bow, and was going away; but Jenny was so much disappointed that Mr. Cullen had made them no present, that she burst into tears.

"What's the matter, my dear?" said Mr. Cullen.

"Oh! nothing at all, sir," cried Jack: "come, Jenny,

don't be so silly; she is only crying about the new gown father had promised her, and the beefsteak pudding and ale for dinner."

"Ay, and father can't pay his rent neither," sobbed Jenny, willing to excuse herself from being thought selfish.

"And why not?" inquired Mr. Cullen.

"Oh, sir, because he is so poor. When he found this purse, he thought the money was all his own, till I rubbed the runners bright, and Jack read your name upon them; and then he said it would be dishonest to keep it."

"That is very true," said Mr. Cullen; "you did quite right to bring back the purse; tell your father that I shall go and see him to-morrow morning, to thank him for restoring the money." Jack again made his bow, and Jenny dropped her courtesy, with as good a grace as she could, when Mr. Cullen chucked her under the chin, and, smiling archly, said, "Beefsteak pudding, was it, lassie; would not beefsteak pie do as well?" Jenny could not understand what he meant; but thinking his joke rather ill-timed, replied, pettishly, "We shan't have either, sir." They then trudged home in sober sadness.

The following morning, Mr. Cullen did not fail to keep his promise of calling at the cottage of the fisherman, and after thanking him for his purse, inquired particularly into his circumstances, and in what way he might be of service to him. He learnt that the ill success of the fishing, which had brought the fisherman into distress, was owing in a great measure to the badness of his nets. He declared that he spent all his spare time in mending them, but that they were so completely worn out that it was almost labour lost.

Mr. Cullen then asked the dame what it was she stood most in need of. She thanked his honour, and said she had a fine large pig, which would serve them for bacon throughout the winter, if she could buy meal to fatten, and salt to cure it; but she had not money for either. Mr. Cullen then turned to the children, and inquired whether they went to school. "No," said the fisherman, "though they have a great desire to go, for some of their playmates go to the school; but I have not the means to send them, for it would be as good as cheating my landlord to pay for my children's schooling, whilst I can't pay my rent."—"Well, do not let that disturb you, my good friend," said Mr. Cullen, "you owe your landlord nothing." The fisherman stared, when Mr. Cullen continued, "I learnt from little Jenny there, that you were at a loss for your rent, and I sent and paid it this morning; you are rent-free to this time twelvemonth. Then, if your children will attend school diligently, I will pay their schooling; what say you?" said he, addressing himself to them.—"Oh! I should never fail," answered Jack, "unless father wanted me to draw the nets; but I could lend a hand at that between school hours." Jenny was vastly pleased, but looked at her mother, who answered for her, that she would be very regular in her attendance; "for," added she, "though it may give me somewhat more to do at home, I am sure in the end it will answer better for myself, as well as the girl, that she should be a bit of a scholar. No one knows, but those who can't read and write, what a thing it is to have a child that can; why, even the little that Jack knows is of great use to us: you see, sir," added the good woman, with great simplicity, "it was Jack found out your name on the runners of the purse. Then, sir, it's a mighty saving to have one's clothes mended neat and strong: we can botch them up after a manner, but the girls at the sewing school would be ashamed of such work; why, they will set you in a patch, that you shan't be able to find it out." Mr. Cullen then took leave, and said they should hear from him again the next day. Accordingly, the next day a cart of Mr. Cullen's drove up to the cottage door, and a variety of things were brought into the house. First there was a sack of meal to fatten the pig, and a bag of salt to cure it; then came a large beefsteak pie, and a small barrel of beer: the children's eyes sparkled with pleasure; but what was their delight when two parcels were opened, in which they found a complete suit of clothes for each of them! The man who drove the cart bade Jenny observe, that the close straw-bonnet, and the warm cloth cloak, were for her to wear in cold weather, to go to church, and to school. Jenny, who dearly loved a little finery, jumped about for joy. Lastly, there was a package of new nets for the fisherman; in short, there was not one of the family that had not cause to rejoice, and be grateful to Mr. Cullen for the kind return he made them for their honesty.

The children improved very much at school. The fisherman and his wife worked hard to do without their aid: the pig was fattened, and, in due time, salted; and the fish when once in the net, finding no holes in it, through which they could escape, were brought safe ashore, and by their sale afforded the family a comfortable maintenance.

LESSON X

ADVERBS OF MANNER

"WE now come to the part of speech called Adverbs: can you guess what that means, Mary?"

"Adverb", repeated Mary, thoughtfully; "that must be something added to a verb—so I suppose it is like an adjective added to a noun, to show what sort of noun it is."

"Something like," replied her mother, "but not quite, for the adverb does not point out the sort of verb; the verb itself shows that. If you say, 'I dance,' or 'He strikes,' the sort of action is described by the verb itself without any adverb being joined to it."

"Then what does the adverb show, mamma?"

"Several things," replied her mother. "In the first place, it shows the manner of the verb. You can read, Mary; but in what manner do you read?"

"Oh, mamma, I hope that I can read well, now that I am seven years old."

"Then *well* is an adverb added to the verb to read. I do not say that it is one which always points out your manner of reading, for sometimes you read *carelessly*."

"Ah, mamma," cried Mary, "that is an adverb, too; and sometimes I read too *fast*: is that an adverb?"

"Yes; and sometimes *indistinctly*."

"Oh, what a number of adverbs there are to describe my manner of reading!" said Mary, laughing.

"I hope you will keep to the first, Mary, and always read *well*; or, if you wish to add other adverbs, let them be to read *slowly, distinctly, fluently*."

"I think, mamma, the adverbs all end in *ly?*"

"Not all. Those that end in *ly* are taken from adjectives: *slow, distinct, fluent*, are adjectives which show the quality of the noun: slow*ly*, distinct*ly*, fluent*ly*, are adverbs which show the manner of the verb. You say, 'A slow horse, A distinct speaker, A fluent tongue, A pretty child:' then, if you add *ly* to those adjectives, you change them into the adverbs *slowly, distinctly, fluently*, and *prettily*, and you add them to verbs instead of to nouns; as he walks *slowly*, she speaks *distinctly*, they read *fluently*, we draw *prettily*."

"Now let me see, mamma, whether I cannot find out an adjective that may be changed into an adverb." She thought a little, then said, "This is a nice cake. Nice is the adjective, and nice*ly* the adverb."

"Yes; you may say it is *nicely* baked. Nice, you see, is the adjective belonging to the noun *cake*, and *nicely* the adverb belonging to the verb *to bake*. I will write down a few adjectives with their corresponding adverbs:—

Dirty	Dirtily
Sweet	Sweetly
Wide	Widely
High	Highly
Fresh	Freshly
New	Newly

"But what does *ly* signify?" inquired Mary; "it changes an adjective into an adverb, and yet it seems to have no meaning."

"It is," said her mother, "an abbreviation of the word *like*; but instead of adding the whole word *like* to the adjectives, which would make them dirtylike, sweetlike, and so on, we add the syllable *ly*, and say dirtily, sweetly."

"Oh then," said Mary, "*ly* is only short for like, and we use it instead of like for that reason. So, then, fresh*ly* means freshlike; high*ly*, highlike; wide*ly*, widelike."

"Oh stop, Mary," cried her mother, interrupting her; "I should not like you to go on with a whole string of adverbs. But observe that the word *like*," continued her mother, "which was many years ago added at full length, is still occasionally used; the Scotch, for instance, say a wise*like* man, and in England we say a lady*like* woman."

"But you do not say gentlemanlike, do you, mamma?" inquired Mary.

"No; I believe it is more common to say gentlemanly."

"Now remember, Mary, that every word which shows you the *manner* in which a verb is done, is an adverb. 'The dog lies quietly.' Can you tell me which is the adverb?"

"Lies," repeated Mary:—"oh no!" continued she, interrupting herself—"lies is doing something, so it must be a verb; but *quietly* is the adverb, because it shows the manner in which the dog lies."

"And which is the adverb in 'John walks fast?'"

"*Fast,*" answered Mary, "because it shows how John walks. Now, mamma, let me think of a sentence. 'The boy spoke civilly, and said he was very sorry to go away.' Can you tell how many adverbs there are there, mamma?"

"Indeed, Mary, you try hard to puzzle me, for there are no less than three adverbs in your sentence; *civilly,* the manner in which the boy spoke; *very,* which shows how sorry he was; and *away,* which shows how he went."

"Oh, mamma!" said Mary, laughing, "then there is one more than I knew of; for I did not think that *away* was an adverb. I wonder," continued she, "that adjectives are not called adnouns; I should remember much more easily what they meant. I shall never forget what adverb means, because the word tells you at once; but I must guess to what an adjective is to be added."

"Very true, my dear; but we cannot take upon ourselves to change the names which grammarians have given to the different parts of speech. Besides, adverbs are not only joined to verbs, but are also sometimes added to adjectives. You remember what an adjective is?"

"Oh yes," replied Mary: "it shows the quality of a thing, and tells you whether it is good or bad, pretty or ugly, small or large." Mary was very fond of going on with a string of examples, so her mamma interrupted her, saying, "That will do, my dear; but observe, that there are many good things which are not all equally good, and many pretty things that are not all equally pretty; in speaking of flowers, for instance, you may say this tulip is rather pretty, but not so pretty as a geranium. Jasmine I think very pretty, and a rose exceedingly pretty. So you see that words are wanted to distinguish the degrees of qualities, and those words are adverbs. Can you tell me which are the adverbs in the phrases I have just used?"

"*Equally, rather, so, very,* and *exceedingly*," replied Mary; "and they must be adverbs of manner, because they show how pretty each of the flowers is."

"Very right," replied her mother; "but observe, that in this sentence the adverbs relate to the manner of the adjective, not to the manner of the verb."

"Oh yes, mamma, I know that pretty is an adjective; but," added she, after some reflection, "I thought that the degrees of comparison of adjectives showed their different degrees of quality?"

"They do; but only when things are compared together, as this orange is sweet, the other is sweeter, and a third is sweetest; but if I want to tell you the degrees of the qualities of a single orange, for instance, one I am eating, I must use adverbs to express them, and say, 'This orange is *very* small, but it is *quite* ripe, and *deliciously* sweet.' Adverbs, when added to adjectives, generally increase the force of the adjective: as a *very* good girl."

"Certainly," said Mary, "a *very* good girl is a stronger expression than a good girl; and a very naughty child is worse than a naughty child."

"I will now write down some of the adverbs of manner," said her mother, "and I expect that at the next lesson you will have introduced them into sentences, to show the manner either of the verb or of the adjective."

Almost	Truly	Uncommonly
Well	Slowly	Wonderfully
Badly	Easily	Extremely
So	Readily	Admirably
Rather		

Mary took great pains with this exercise, and introduced the adverbs in the following manner:—

"I am *almost* ready.

That is *well* written.

It is *badly* spelt.

He is *so* angry.

I am *rather* tired.

He spoke *truly*.

She reads *slowly*.

They dance *easily*.

You talk *readily*.

An *uncommonly* large apple.

A *wonderfully* wise man.

An *extremely* pretty doll.

An *admirably* good lesson."

"You see, mamma," said Mary, "that the nine first adverbs are added to verbs, and the four last to adjectives."

Her mother was much pleased, and praised her diligence and attention.

LESSON XI

ADVERBS OF TIME AND PLACE

At the next lesson, Mary's mother told her that there were several other classes of adverbs for her to learn.

"When you know the manner in which a verb is done, you may also wish to know the place where it was done. If you heard that little Sophy had fallen down and hurt herself, you might inquire *where* she had fallen down, and *where* she had hurt herself: and she might point with her finger to the place where she had fallen, and say *here*; then she might point to the spot where she had hurt herself, and say *there*. Thus, you see, *here*, *there*, and *where*, are adverbs."

"Yes; but they are not adverbs of manner," observed Mary.

"True: cannot you find out what sort of adverbs they are by their meaning?"

Mary thought for some time, and then said, "*Here* means in this place; *there* means in that place; and *where* means in what place? They all show the place in which the verb is done, so I suppose they are called adverbs of place. Have I guessed right, mamma?"

"You have done better than guessed, my dear, you have reasoned right."

"And yet," said Mary, "the name of a place is a noun, so how can it be an adverb?"

"Observe," said her mother, "that the adverb does not name the place, but points it out without naming it. If Sophy, in answer to your inquiries, had said, 'I fell on the *steps*, and I have hurt my *head*,' *head* and *steps* are nouns; but if she said, I fell *there*, and hurt my head *here*, *here* and *there* are adverbs."

"Then adverbs of place are like pronouns, I think," said Mary, "for they are put instead of the name of the place."

"There is a considerable resemblance, it is true," replied her mother; "but words which point out the place are always classed as adverbs, not as pronouns."

"Pray, mamma, let me try to find out some adverbs of place. I thought I had put my thimble *there*," said she, opening her work-box, "but," added she, looking about, "I am seeking for it *every where*, and I can find it *nowhere*."

"Well then," said her mother, "if you cannot find it *here*, you must search for it *elsewhere*, for it must be *somewhere*, though you say you cannot find it *any where*. But I conclude this is only an example you are supposing, and that you have not really lost your thimble."

"Oh no! *here* it is," said Mary, laughing, and showing it on her finger; "it is not lost."

"Then remember, Mary, that every word which

points out the place in which a verb is performed, without naming it, is an adverb of place. Now for the third class of adverbs. When you know the manner in which the verb is done, and the place where it was done, is there nothing more you would like to know about it?"

"I think not," replied Mary.

"Well," said her mother, "I am going to Ash Grove, and I can easily make room for you in the carriage, if you like to go. Now you know the manner of going, and the place I am going to, are you satisfied?"

"Oh, I should like to go of all things," cried Mary, "but I am not yet satisfied, for I want to know when you will go; I hope it will be soon."

"What does *soon* mean, my dear?"

"It means in a very short time."

"Then *soon* points out the time at which the verb is to be performed, and is called an adverb of time." Her mother then gave her the following list of adverbs of time.

Now	Before	Afterwards
Directly	Soon	Then
Immediately	Presently	Never
Instantly	By and by	Always
Already		

"*Now*, means the present time," said Mary.

"And so does *directly*, *instantly*, and *immediately*," observed her mother.

"But," rejoined Mary, "if you bid me do something, and I answer I will do it directly, or immediately, or instantly, I mean as soon as possible; but I cannot do it whilst I am speaking, so those words cannot express the present time so exactly as *now* does."

"Yes they do; but we are accustomed to use them incorrectly, as we do many other words, and even the word *now*. How often do you say, '*now* I will go out,' meaning to go out as soon as you have finished speaking, but not whilst you are speaking?"

"Then the adverb *before* puzzles me," said Mary, "for I thought it was a preposition; if you say, 'John, walk *before* the horse,' *before* must be a preposition, because it shows the connection between the two nouns, John and horse."

"*Before*," replied her mother, "like many other words, belongs to two parts of speech, according to its meaning in the sentence. If you say I never saw him *before*, or you told me so *before*, in both these sentences *before* relates to him, and is an adverb. But if you say, the man stood *before* the door, or the prisoner was brought *before* the judge, they are prepositions, denoting the connection between prisoner and judge."

"I suppose," said Mary, "that *after* is an adverb, as well as *before?*"

83

"No," replied her mother; "*after* is always a preposition, the corresponding adverb of time is *afterwards*."

"I am glad of that," said Mary, "this distinction makes them more easy to understand."

Mary then introduced some of the adverbs of time into the following sentence. "I am tired *now*, but I shall *soon* be rested, and *then* I shall be able to play again. Ann will be here *directly*, and Charles will come *afterwards*. Susan is here *already*, she *always* comes *first*."

"The next class of adverbs," said her mother, "expresses the number of times the verb is performed; as I spoke *once*, or *twice*, or *thrice*."

"Then," said Mary, "are one, two, three, four, and all the numbers, adverbs?"

"No," replied her mother; "I shall explain them to you later; but they cannot be adverbs, because they relate to the noun, not to the verb; you say one apple, ten houses, fifty men, and so on; but you do not say, I wrote *one*, but I wrote *once*; because *once* relates to the verb, and not to the noun."

"Well," said Mary, "I do think so many different sorts of adverbs is a little puzzling. First, there are adverbs of manner, to tell you *how* something was done; then adverbs of place, to show *where* it was done; then adverbs of time, to say *when* it was done; and, lastly, adverbs of number, to point out *how often* it was done."

"Not lastly," said her mother, "for there are several other classes of adverbs;" then, observing Mary look grave, she added, "do not be alarmed, I shall not teach you any more of them to-day. But I must observe," continued she, "that if adverbs are, in some respects, a difficult part of speech, yet, in others, they are easier than nouns or pronouns, as they have neither person, number, nor gender; but you have had enough of them to-day; so go and take a run in the garden to refresh yourself."

OTHER CLASSES OF ADVERBS

"In order to be able to recollect all the different sorts of adverbs, my dear," said Mary's mother to her, "you must class them in regular order in your memory."

"Yes," said Mary, "I must put them in order in my head, as I do my doll's clothes in her chest of drawers."

"Very well," replied her mother, smiling at the comparison, "and put each class in a separate drawer."

"How droll," said Mary, laughing, "that my head should be like a chest of drawers!"

"I hope it is like a tidy chest of drawers, Mary: I have known some little girls whose drawers were in such confusion, that when they wanted any thing in them, they did not know in which drawer to look for it; and, when that is the case," added she, looking archly at Mary, "I cannot help suspecting that their heads are in the same sort of confusion."

"Yes; but I do not think you know such a little girl just now, mamma, for, if you recollect, you praised me the other day for having my drawers in such tidy order."

"Well, then, it is to be hoped, Mary, that I shall find your head so too. Now, let us see how many drawers you must have to keep the adverbs in. Do you recollect how many we have already mentioned?"

"Let me see," said Mary, thinking; "why, first, I must have a drawer, and a pretty large one, for the adverbs relating to the *manner* of the verb, there are so many of them; such as *prettily, cleverly, nicely.* Then another for adverbs relating to *place;* as *here, there, every where.* Then a third drawer for adverbs relating to time; as *now, then, presently.* That need not be so large a drawer I believe: and, lastly, a little tiny drawer will be enough for the adverbs that relate to number; as *once, twice, thrice, and away,*" said she; and then set off with a hop, skip, and a jump, and ran to the other end of the room—an exercise which never failed to relieve her mind when weary of thinking.

"But, my dear," said her mother, "you know that we have not finished the adverbs; there are several other classes for you to learn."

"Then I must have some more drawers to put them in; and pray what are they?"

"The next class of adverbs relates to the quantity of the verb; as 'You have played *enough;* he has eaten *sufficiently.*'"

"Let me try," said Mary. " 'I have worked *much* longer than I intended. He danced *less* than you did.' "

"Another class of adverbs asks questions," said her

mother; "as, '*How* do you do? *What* do you say? *Why* should we go? *When* shall we set out?'"

"Oh yes, I know those are questions, because there is a note of interrogation; but what has that to do with a verb?"

"In the sentence '*How* do you do?' *how* relates to the verb to do, and means, 'How does your health do?' In '*What* do you say?' *what* relates to the verb to say, and so on."

Mary inquired whether there were any adverbs that answered questions.

"Yes, there are," replied her mother, "especially two little words that you are very fond of."

Mary wondered what they could be.

"Suppose I were to ask you whether you have read to-day, what would you answer?"

"I should say '*Yes;*' for I have read a long chapter in the History of England, with Miss Thompson."

"But supposing that you had not read to-day?"

"Then I should say, 'No.'"

"Well, then, *yes* and *no* are adverbs, and so are all other words that reply to a question; such as, *perhaps, surely, certainly, by no means, not at all.*"

"But, mamma," said Mary, "how can *yes* and *no* be adverbs, for they cannot relate to any verb?"

"I beg your pardon: if you say *yes*, in answer to my question, 'Have you read?' you mean to say, 'Yes, I have read:' you see, therefore, that *yes* by itself refers to the verb to read; it is understood, though the verb is not mentioned. Try to introduce some of the adverbs I have mentioned by asking questions, to which they will serve as answers."

Mary thought a little, and then wrote as follows:—

" 'Will you walk to-day?'

" '*Perhaps*, if the weather is fine.'

" 'Are you hungry?'

" '*Certainly;* it is dinner-time.'

" 'Are you tired?'

" '*No, not at all.*'

" 'Are you glad to see me?

" '*Yes, surely.*'

" 'Are you tired of play?'

" '*No, by no means.*' "

"Very well," said her mother: "and you have already done what I was going to teach you, that is, used two adverbs instead of one; as, *yes, surely; no, by no means:* this is frequently done, and strengthens the expression. I will give you some examples: 'Ann speaks *very distinctly*. John draws *extremely well*. Charles walks *too slowly.*' "

Mary was never satisfied till she had found out some examples herself, so she said, " 'George writes *exceedingly ill*. Ann coughs *very badly*. Susan laughs *too much.*' "

"Some adverbs," said her mother, "have degrees of comparison; as often, *oftener, oftenest*; well, *better, best.*"

"But, mamma," cried Mary, interrupting her, "you said that good, better, best, were adjectives."

"Good," replied she, "is always an adjective; but better and best are sometimes adjectives, and sometimes adverbs."

"Oh, that is very puzzling; and in my parsing lessons how am I to find out whether they are adjectives or adverbs?"

"By observing whether they relate to nouns or to verbs. If I say, 'I spoke *well,* you spoke *better,* but Henry spoke *best,*' the words *well, better, best,* are adverbs, because they relate to the verb to speak; but if you say, 'A *good* child, a *better* child, the *best* child,' the degrees of comparison relate to the noun child, and are, therefore, adjectives."

"Yes; and then you must say *good,* instead of *well,* for it would be nonsense to say a *well* child."

"Whenever," said her mother, "the two degrees of comparison, better and best, are used as adverbs, the positive is *well;* and when they are used as adjectives, the positive is *good.*"

"Let me find out an example, mamma; first, for adjectives—'I am a *good* dancer, Sophy is a *better* dancer, but Ellen dances *best.*'"

"Stop," said her mother: "there is a mistake in your example: try if you can find it out."

Mary repeated the phrase slowly and deliberately, but she thought in vain, and could not discover the fault. "What can it be, mamma?" said she.

"In the two first degrees of comparison," replied her mother, "you are right; but when you said, 'Ellen dances best,' the word *best* relates to the verb *dances*, and not to the noun *dancer*."

"To be sure," said Mary, "I did not think of that; a *dancer* is a person and a noun; while *dances* is a verb. I ought to have said Ellen is the best dancer. And is it wrong to mix the adjectives and the adverbs so in one sentence?"

"Not at all," replied her mother. "Adverbs," continued she, "are sometimes joined to verbs, so as to make one word; as, to *upset*, to *undertake*, to *outdo*, to *overlay*."

"And are such words adverbs or verbs?" inquired Mary.

"They are considered as verbs, for they all express an action. Now, Mary, I believe that we have gone through as many of the different classes of adverbs as it will be necessary for you to learn at present; do you think that you can recollect them all?"

"I will try, mamma. An adverb is a word added to a verb to show something that relates to it; 1st, The manner of the verb; as, 'he speaks *well*.' 2dly, The place of the verb; as, 'Ellen came *here*.' 3dly, The time of the verb; as, 'I write *now*.' 4thly, The number of the verb; as, 'They drank *twice*.' 5thly, The quantity of the verb; as, *little, much, more*. 6thly, Adverbs that ask questions; as,

'*What* shall we do?' 7thly, Those which answer questions; as, '*Yes,*' '*No.*' Dear me, what an immense deal adverbs do! They show *how*, and *when*, and *where*, and *how much*, and *how often*, a verb is done; and then besides that, they ask and answer questions. Oh, but, mamma, I must have two more drawers for my questions and answers, for you know I did not reckon them in my chest of drawers."

"Very true," said her mother. "I think we may now take leave of adverbs; and for to-morrow I have prepared a story instead of a lesson."

Mary was pleased to hear this: for though she now liked her lessons of grammar very well, she liked the stories still better.

A STORY

THE SPONGE CAKES

Mrs. Burton was one day walking in the fields with her little daughter Harriet, who skipped on before her through the grass. The gay flowers sprung up beneath her feet, and smelt very sweet; but she did not stop to gather them, for she was impatient to reach the village where they were going to the pastry-cook's. Harriet had sixpence of her own to lay out, and all the way she went she was thinking what sort of cakes she would buy. For herself she liked plum buns, but she meant also to buy a cake for her little sister Fanny, and she was not sure what she would like best.

On their way they stopped at Mrs. Spruce's (the washerwoman's) cottage, as Mrs. Burton had some directions to give her. Mrs. Spruce had a pretty little daughter, called Alice, who often accompanied her mother when she carried home Mrs. Burton's linen from washing, and then Harriet and Alice sometimes played together; so Harriet was very glad to call at the cottage to see Alice, and she ran forward, and opening the little garden-gate, called out, "Alice! Alice!" but no Alice answered. When they went in, they saw poor Alice sitting quite still in a low chair, and looking so pale and ill that she seemed as if she had not strength to move.

"What is the matter with poor Alice?" inquired Mrs. Burton.

"Indeed, ma'am, I can't say," replied Mrs. Spruce. "She has been in this downcast way for this week and more. The doctor calls it a sort of low fever; but no wonder she is so weak, for I can get her to eat nothing. The only thing she fancies is a bit of sponge cake. A lady gave her one last Wednesday, but it is all gone, and I cannot afford to buy her any more."

"Does the doctor think it good for her to eat sponge cake?" inquired Mrs. Burton.

"He says it will do her no harm if she wishes it."

Soon after Mrs. Burton and her little daughter left the cottage, and, as they walked on towards the village, they could talk of nothing but poor Alice. When they reached the pastry-cook's, Mrs. Burton asked Harriet if she had made up her mind what she should buy?

"Oh yes, mamma, sponge cakes;" and she inquired how many she could have for sixpence. She was told six; and six sponge cakes were put up in a piece of paper and given to her, and she paid for them.

"I thought, my dear," said her mother, "that you intended to buy plum buns?"

"So I did, mamma; but I have bought these cakes for poor Alice: she can eat nothing else, you know, while I am hungry for every thing. So it is much better for Alice to have the cakes, than for me to have buns."

"You are a good child," said her mother, giving her a kind kiss, "to think what will please others rather than yourself. But then, little Fanny—will she like to go without her cake? She is too young to care about Alice."

"Oh, she does not know any thing about the cake, mamma, for I did not tell her I should give her one; I meant to surprise her, so she will not be disappointed."

When they drew near the cottage, on their way home, Harriet hastened forward, pushed open the garden-gate, and was soon in the house. She then opened her little parcel, and gave one of the cakes to Alice. Poor Alice smiled, and, though it was but faintly, Harriet was delighted to see her face, which was before so melancholy, look pleased. Alice tasted a little bit, and said it was very good, but she would not eat much, saying she would keep the rest for another time.

"Oh, here are a great many more cakes," said Harriet eagerly, "and they are all for you, Alice."

"How good you are, my dear young lady," said Mrs. Spruce; "you have made poor Alice quite happy."

Harriet felt quite happy too: she was much happier than if she had eaten the cakes herself; she was so glad to do some good to poor Alice. In her way home she gathered a quantity of field flowers. "I shall give some of them to Fanny," said she, "instead of the cake, and then she will be pleased too." Harriet liked to please every one, but she herself was the happiest of all, because she enjoyed making others happy.

95

LESSON XIII

PREPOSITIONS

AT the next lesson Mary's mother asked her what the grammar said about prepositions.

"Prepositions!" repeated Mary, "what a long, hard word!" Her mother took up the book and pointed out the place to Mary, who read as follows:—

"Prepositions serve to connect nouns together, and to show the relation between them."

"I do not know what relation means," continued she, "unless it is like uncle and aunt Howard, and my cousins, who are all our relations."

"They are called our relations," replied her mother, "because they belong to the same family that we do; but the relation between words is not quite the same thing. The relation between two nouns means what one of the nouns has to do with the other. You will understand it if I give you an example. Here is a table, that is a noun; and there is a chair, that is another noun. Now, if I say, 'Put the chair *by* the table,' *by* is the preposition which shows the relation between the table and the chair. If

I left out the preposition, and said, 'Put the chair the table,' you could not understand what I meant."

"No, indeed, mamma, for it would be nonsense; but the little word *by* explains it all very clearly."

"Now," said her mother, "can you tell me what relation there is between this book and the table?"

"The book does not stand *by* the table like the chair," said Mary; "it lies *on* the table."

"And which is the preposition?"

Mary thought a little, and then replied, "The book lies—no, it is not lies, for lies is the verb—it is what the book does:" then she suddenly exclaimed, *"on* the table—yes, *on* is the word which shows the relation between the book and the table."

"You are right," said her mother. "Now, where is the footstool?"

"It is under the table," answered Mary; "and I guess that *under* is a preposition. Now, mamma, I run round the table; is not *round* a preposition also?"

"Yes, it is, when used in that sense; but if you said, 'That is a round table,' *round* would not, in that case, show the relation of the table to any thing else; so *round* would not then be a preposition."

"Oh, but I know what it would be, mamma, it would be an adjective; for it would show what sort of a table it was."

Mary, having run once or twice round the table, placed one of her feet upon the footstool, and, springing up, seated herself upon the table. "Now, mamma," said she, "what is the preposition that connects me with the table?"

"*On*, or *upon*, which you like best; but I fear that my table may suffer from your frolics, so you had better come down and sit in a chair *near* the table."

"Oh, yes: *near* is a preposition:" and she seated herself on the side of the table, opposite to her mother, who said, "Here, Mary, catch this ball of worsted which I am going to throw *over* the table."

Mary caught it, and asked how *over* could be a preposition, for the ball had not touched the table, nor been near it.

"That is true," replied her mother, "yet *over* shows the relation between the ball and the table; the table was underneath while the ball went over it. The chair which stands by the table does not necessarily touch it; nor does the footstool, which is under the table."

"Well, I am sure this is a very useful table; for do not you remember, mamma, it taught me all about adjectives, and now it teaches me all about prepositions?"

"True," replied her mother; "but let us try our prepositions on something else besides the table. There is a man walking across the street; can you find out the preposition?"

"Let me see; it is *across*—yes, across shows the relation between the two nouns, man and street. Now he is going into that house, mamma. Oh!" cried she, pleased at the discovery, "*into* is a preposition between man and house; and now he is gone *up* stairs, for see, he is looking out of the window. But, mamma, is *up* a preposition? for there is only one noun in the sentence, 'he is gone up stairs.'"

"Who was it went up stairs, my dear?"

"Oh, the man, to be sure; but I did not say the man."

"No, but you said, 'he went up stairs;' what did *he* mean?"

"'He is the pronoun put instead of the noun *man*, that is true."

"And it is just the same as if you said, 'the man went up stairs.'"

"So, then, a preposition shows the relation between a noun and a pronoun, as well as between two nouns?"

"Certainly, or between two pronouns—*you* stand *by me*. You and me are both pronouns, and *by* shows their relation to each other."

"He speaks to her," said Mary: "*to* is the preposition which relates to the pronouns *he* and *her*."

"Prepositions are easy enough when you know what they mean; but one is frightened at first by the long hard name."

"However, you soon get accustomed to it," replied her mother. "The name comes from two Latin words *before* and *place*, as prepositions are generally placed before nouns."

"No, mamma, a preposition is placed between two nouns."

"Then it must stand before one of them, Mary?"

"Yes; but if you say that a preposition is placed before a noun, you might mistake an article for a preposition, for an article, you know, always stands before a noun."

"True, my dear, but the articles are so few in number that there is not much danger of confounding them with prepositions."

"I think, mamma," said Mary, "that prepositions always mean something about place; as *in* the box, *under* the chair, *through* the hole, all relate to the places where the box, the chair, and the hole are."

"It is true," said her mother, "prepositions very generally denote the relation of place, but not always. This curtain is made *of* silk, that bonnet is *for* you; now, *of* and *for* do not relate to place."

"Yes," replied Mary, "but I think almost all the other prepositions do. *Along* the road, *down* the valley, *up* the hill, *across* the river."

"And several of these prepositions, you know, Mary, are used as adverbs; when you say sit *down*, get *up*, go *along*, those three prepositions become adverbs."

"And how am I to know when they are prepositions and when adverbs?" said Mary.

By observing whether they point out a relation between nouns and pronouns, or are simply added to a verb. 'Pour some water on your hands, go on, there is not enough yet.' Now can you distinguish which *on* is a preposition, and which is an adverb?"

"The first, I am sure, is a preposition," said Mary, "because it shows the connection between the water and my hands, and the second is an adverb, added to the verb go; I cannot mistake it, because it has nothing to do with a noun. Now," continued she, "I will try an example, 'I will get *up* and go *up* stairs;' the first *up* is an adverb belonging to the verb get; and the last *up* is a preposition, showing the connection between me and the stairs."

"Very well," said her mother. "Prepositions are sometimes joined to nouns, as *underground, overboard.*"

"Just as adverbs are joined to verbs," observed Mary. "Then what part of speech are those words, mamma; nouns or prepositions?"

"Try to discover, yourself, my dear; though I must tell you that they are neither nouns nor prepositions."

"To be sure," said Mary, "it would be nonsense to say *the* underground, *an* overboard, so they cannot be nouns; but you may say the gardener digs underground, or the man fell overboard. Oh! I have guessed mamma; they are adverbs, for they are joined to verbs."

"You are quite right, my dear," said her mother; but *underground* is sometimes an adjective also, for we may talk of an underground cavern. We will now finish the lesson, and to-morrow we may proceed to conjunctions."

LESSON XIV

CONJUNCTIONS

"Conjunctions are words which have not much meaning in themselves, but serve the purpose of joining words or parts of sentences together. If I say, 'Bring me a pen and some writing-paper,' the sentence consists of two parts joined together by the little word *and*."

"Oh, yes, I understand," said Mary—"the first part of the sentence is 'Bring me a pen,' and the second part, 'some writing-paper;' and the little word *and* joins them both together, and so it is called a conjunction. Now, mamma, let me try to think of a sentence:" then after a pause, she said, "I will fetch my doll *and* her cradle!" then she suddenly exclaimed, "Why, mamma, how very like conjunctions are to prepositions! You know that a preposition shows the relation between two nouns, and the conjunction *and* seems to me to do just the same thing, for it shows the relation between pen and paper, and between my doll and her cradle."

"No, Mary, it joins the words, but it does not show how they are related to each other. When I say, 'Bring me a pen and some writing-paper,' I mean nothing more than that you should bring me those two things; but I do not point out any relation between them."

"Oh, but you know, mamma, I must think you are going to write, and then I am sure there is a great connection between the pen and the paper."

"You may think what you please, my dear," said her mother, smiling: "but there is no relationship between them pointed out by the little word *and*. If I had said, 'Bring me a pen *on* the writing-paper, or *in* the writing-paper,' that would show a relation, for the pen was to be placed *in* or *on* the paper."

"Oh, yes," said Mary; "and if I said I will bring my doll *in* her cradle, instead of *and* her cradle, I should say a preposition instead of a conjunction."

"Besides," said her mother, "*and* is not only used to join nouns together, but verbs also, and any two parts of a sentence whatever: thus I may say, 'Bring your book, *and* come *and* read.' There is the noun book in the first part of the sentence, and the latter part consists of two verbs."

"And then are two conjunctions, mamma, for the two verbs are also joined by *and*."

"Yes, you know I told you that conjunctions served to join words as well as sentences together. But we have talked a great deal about the word *and*, Mary, without mentioning any other conjunction. You may play with your doll *if* you please."

"Oh, yes; *if* joins the two parts of the sentence quite as well as *and*, and seems to have more meaning in it."

103

"There are a great many more conjunctions," said her mother: "I will ride *or* I will walk. I shall drive to Highgate, *but* not to Hampstead."

"I will go with you, mamma, *if* you will let me. I hope it is true, and not merely playing at finding out conjunctions."

"Well, my dear, to-morrow, perhaps, you may, *but* you must now think only of your lesson, *for*, unless you are very attentive, you can *neither* go to Hampstead *nor* to Highgate."

"What a number of conjunctions!" exclaimed Mary.

"Observe," said her mother, "the change which different conjunctions make in the meaning of the sentence: if, instead of saying, 'I will give you an orange *and* an apple,' I should say, 'I will give you an orange *or* an apple ...'"

"Oh! I like the conjunction *and* much the best, for it joins the real apple and the orange together, as well as the words, and then you give me both."

"But I might also take from you an apple, or an orange, and then I think you would prefer *or* to *and*."

"Oh, yes! that I should," said Mary, laughing.

"Now these conjunctions," continued her mother, "which join things or actions together, are called *copulative conjunctions;* and those which separate or disjoin them are called *disjunctive conjunctions*."

"Oh dear, what long words!" exclaimed Mary.

"When I say, 'You may *either* ride or walk,' what sort of conjunction is *either?*"

"Disjunctive," said Mary, "because it disjoins walking and riding; for it means that I may do one or the other, but not both. But how can a conjunction both join and disjoin things at the same time. I think if I told you that I could join and disjoin things at the same time, you would say, 'Oh, Mary, you are talking nonsense.'"

"You must distinguish between things and words," replied her mother: "a conjunction always joins the words or the parts of which the sentence is composed, but it does not always join the things or the actions the sentence talks about."

"Oh, yes," said Mary, "it joins the two words *walk* and *ride*, but it does not join the two things *walking* and *riding*."

"I see that you understand it, Mary, but you do not express it quite correctly. You should not say, the two things, but the two actions, for you know that walking and riding are verbs, not nouns, and therefore cannot be things."

"Yes," said Mary, "they are actions and an action means doing the verb. Now, let me find out some disjunctive conjunctions. Sophy will *neither* eat *nor* drink: those are disjunctive conjunctions; but if I say, she both eats *and* drinks, the conjunction *and* is copulative, because it joins the actions eating and drinking, as well as the words eat and drink."

"Very well; or you might say, Sophy will eat *as well as*

drink." Her mother then wrote a list of the conjunctions she could recollect.

And	But	Perhaps
If	Either	Unless
Or	Neither	Because
Nor	Though	

"I think we may now take leave of conjunctions, and to-morrow we will proceed to interjections.

LESSON XV

INTERJECTIONS

"THIS part of speech can hardly be called words; for it consists of exclamations, or cries, uttered by a person who admires, or is surprised or frightened, such as oh! ah! alas! Oh dear me! They are very easy to find out for they are always written with a line and a dot after them, called a note of admiration."

Interjections amused Mary extremely: she remembered an old nurse who used to sigh and say, "Heigh ho!" and "Alack and a well-a-day!" and asked whether those were interjections. Her mother told her they were.

"But, mamma," said Mary, "nurse used to say so, very often, without admiring any thing, or being surprised or frightened."

"Very aged people," said her mother, "are apt to use exclamations of that sort from a feeling of weariness, without thinking; and some very young people acquire the same habit from the vivacity and impatience of youth. How often you say, 'Oh yes!' and 'Oh dear no!' when simple yes or no would have done as well."

"Perhaps they would," said Mary; "but I like much better saying oh! and ah!"

"Then," said her mother, "you should tell me what it is that frightens or delights you."

"It is only make-believe, mamma."

"Then make-believe to be frightened or delighted with something."

Mary thought a little, and then said, "Oh! I am afraid that horse will gallop over me!"

"And now for an exclamation of pleasure," said her mother.

"Oh! you are to tell me a long story tomorrow, mamma; and, when I have heard it, I shall use an interjection of admiration, and say, 'O dear! how pretty it is!' "

"Well, I see that we must come to the story at last;" and the next day she read as follows:—

A STORY

THE CRUST OF BREAD

A Fairy Tale

EDWARD, a little boy six years old, was one day strolling about the garden, eating a large crust of bread: he threw himself on the grass, and lay idly basking in the sun without thinking of any thing. All at once there appeared before him a beautiful fairy, whose name was Instruction. Her dress shone with the brilliant colours of the rainbow, and she wore a crown of flowers on her head. In one hand she held a silver wand, with which she could perform wonderful things, and in the other, a book, the leaves of which were all made of looking-glass, and which was no less wonderful than the wand. She smiled and looked so good-humouredly on Edward, that instead of being frightened he was quite pleased. She then opened and showed him her book. In the first page he saw himself and every thing around him reflected as you do in a common looking-glass; but the other pages were of a very wonderful nature, for they reflected objects which were quite out of sight, and even in the most remote parts of the world. In one page he beheld lions and tigers in Africa roaming about in search of prey. Edward shrunk back half frightened at seeing them move and look alive; but the fairy explained to him that it was only the image of a wild beast, just as the image of his face was represented in the first page; so that there was really nothing to fear.

She then turned over another leaf; and Edward saw a large elephant in India, tearing up a young tree by the roots with his trunk. In another page she showed him the monkeys climbing up the trees in the woods in America, and hanging by their tails to the branches, gibbering and pelting each other with nuts: while the parrots, with their gaudy plumage, flew about as common as sparrows do here. The fairy now closed her book. Edward begged of her to show him a few more of the looking-glass leaves, and declared that he had never seen any picture-book half so pretty as this; but the fairy said there were so many children wanting to see it, that she could not stay with him any longer.

"Oh dear," cried Edward, "what shall I do when you are gone, and nothing to amuse me?"

"You seemed very well amused before I came," said the fairy, "lounging as you were on the grass, and eating your crust of bread."

"So I was," replied Edward; "but since you have shown me that pretty book I shall do nothing but long to see it again. I don't care for my crust of bread any longer."

"Well," said the fairy. "I will make you care for your bread again. I will give the bread the power of speaking, and it shall tell you its history, from beginning to end; will not that amuse you?"

"Yes, indeed, it will," replied Edward: "it will be so strange to hear the crust of bread speak."

"Take care to hold it to your ear, and not to your mouth," said the fairy, smiling; "for were you thoughtlessly to give it a bite whilst it was speaking, it would tell you no more." She then waved her wand over the bread and disappeared.

When she was gone, Edward began to think she must have been joking; however, he took up the bread and held it to his ear. He started back with surprise, when he heard a small gentle voice speak as follows:—

"The first thing I can remember was when I was only a grain of corn, lying in a large room, with a great many other grains. We remained there a long time; when one day a man came and took out a quantity of us. He put us into a sack and carried us to a field that had just been ploughed, and there he took us out of the sack and strewed us in handsfull on the ground."

"That was sowing corn," said Edward.

"I shall never forget," continued the bread, "how sweet and fresh the newly-ploughed earth smelt, and how much I enjoyed lying there with the warm sunbeams shining on me. Soon after there came by a flight of crows; and the labourers being away, they alighted on the ground and began picking up all the grains of corn within their reach. I lay trembling with alarm, thinking my turn would come, and that I too should be devoured; but before they reached the spot where I was, the labourers returned to the field, and frightened them away. Soon after there was a shower of rain, and some of the drops fell upon me, and carried me down with them into the ground, where I was quite safe from the birds. There I remained some time: but I found that I began to swell and grow so large that at last my skin could not hold me, so it burst open, and out there came at one end a little tuft of small roots scarcely larger than hairs; these struck into the ground and grew downwards. At the other end out came several tiny green stalks, which grew above the ground. At first they looked like blades of grass; but they soon became taller and taller, and stronger and stronger, and at last a beautiful ear of corn was seen at the top and a few long leaves, like those of grass, grew on the sides of each stalk. Thus from a small seed of corn I was changed into a little plant; and a very pretty change it was. The little roots sucked in water, which went up all through my green veins into the ears, and made them swell out and grow large and full of seeds. Then, when the hot weather came, the sun turned us as yellow as gold, and the wind blew us about with the other ears of corn that grew in the same field, and I assure you we all felt very proud of our grace and beauty. But our pride did not last long; for one day a number of men came into the field with sickles, and cut us all down."

"Those were the reapers," said Edward.

"We were then bound up in sheaves and set upright on the ground, leaning one against the other for support: for, being separated from our roots in the ground, we

112

were no longer able to stand upright. We remained some days and nights on the ground, and then we were put into a large cart and carried to the rick-yard to be stacked; there we were left quietly for some time, except that a frightful rat now and then found its way into the stack, and made great havoc amongst us, devouring as many of us as he could swallow for his breakfast. After some time a number of men came again and pulled us down, and, spreading us upon the floor of a barn, began beating us most unmercifully."

"Those were the thrashers," said Edward; "it was well for you that you could not feel, for those double sticks they use, called flails, give very hard blows."

"It was indeed," replied the crust of bread. "Well, these hard blows drove us all out of the ears in which we grew. The stalks, which were then nothing but straw, were taken away; but the grains of corn, with the chaff were put into a large flat basket and shaken about till the chaff was all blown away, and nothing but the grains remained."

"So, then you were changed back again into a grain of corn," said Edward.

"Not into one grain," replied the bread, "but into one or two hundred. I was but a single grain, it is true, when I was first sown in the ground, but I sprung up with so many fine ears that I do believe I had above two hundred seeds; no others were so plump and well-grown as ourselves. Well, the next thing that happened to us was being sent to the mill to be ground all to pieces to make flour; and after that to the baker, who mixed us up with water and yeast, and made us into a piece of dough, and after we had been well kneaded, he put us into an oven to bake. We thus became part of a loaf of bread, which the baker's boy brought here to-day to be eaten."

At the last word the voice failed—the power of the fairy's wand was at an end. Edward waited for some time to listen whether the bread would say anything more; and finding it quite silent, he took it from his ear, put it to his mouth, and ate it up.

LESSON XVI

PARSING, PART I

"To-day, Mary," said her mother, "I will teach you an amusing way of finding out the parts of speech. I shall give you a sentence, leaving out one word, and you must discover to what part of speech the word left out belongs. I shall make a pause to show you in what part of the sentence the unknown word is to be placed."

"Oh, mamma!" cried Mary, "how will it be possible for me to tell the part of speech, unless I know what the word is?"

"It is not so difficult as you imagine," replied her mother. "Here is an example: 'Put the doll ——— her bed.'"

"No, indeed! that is quite easy," said Mary; "I am sure the word must be *in* her bed, and *in* is a preposition."

"I did not ask you to find out the word, my dear, but to make out the part of speech."

"But surely I must first know the word," said Mary.

"That is not at all necessary," replied her mother; "and you are perhaps mistaken in the one you have guessed."

"Well then, if it is not *in*," said Mary, "it must be *on* her bed, or *near*, or *by* her bed, and *on* and *near* and *by* are all prepositions, because they show the relation between the doll and her bed."

"Therefore," observed her mother, "if you had said that the unknown word was a preposition, you would have been right; but it is mere guess-work to say which of the prepositions it is."

"Now I understand it," said Mary; "so pray, mamma, let me give you a word to find out; but I must consider what it shall be, for I will not give you another preposition—you would guess that directly." Then, after reflecting a little, she said, "There is a ⸺ child:" and when she paused she gave a little "hem!" to mark the place of the unknown word more distinctly.

"Your unknown word must describe the sort of child," said her mother; "therefore it is an adjective."

"Oh! but pray, mamma, guess whether it is pretty, or little, or good, or naughty, or clean, or dirty, or dark, or fair; or any thing else."

"All these adjectives have about an equal chance of being the one you have chosen, Mary; and as you have mentioned no less than eight, it is seven to one whether I guess right; and if I should, it is but mere guess-work after all."

"Well, if you positively will not guess, mamma, I must tell you it was *little* child."

"If I had guessed, then," replied her mother, "I should

have guessed wrong, for I should have said pretty, as I know you are very fond of pretty children."

"Now, pray, let me give you another word without a name," said Mary, "it is such good fun. But I must try to think of something difficult, you find it out so easily; 'May I go —— the garden, and —— a nosegay.' There are two words for you to make out, and they are not the same parts of speech, so I hope, mamma, I have set you a good hard task."

"I must take great pains," replied her mother, "to make no mistake. I and the garden, Mary, are two nouns."

"Oh no, mamma, *I* is a pronoun."

"True, but the pronoun stands for the noun, so it comes to the same thing. Well, the unknown word must point out the relation between the word *I* and the garden, therefore it must be a preposition; whether you ask leave to go *through* the garden, or *by* the garden, or *in* the garden, I cannot tell; but at all events it must be a preposition. Then I suppose I am to do something to a nosegay, so that unknown word must be a verb, whether I am to smell it, or wear it, or look at it, or gather it."

"There you have guessed it, mamma; the two words are *in* and *gather;* but, as you say, any person ever so stupid, and who knows nothing of grammar, may *guess* at the word as well as you, mamma, the difficulty is in making out the part of speech."

"And in order to do that," continued her mother, "you must have some knowledge of grammar, and sufficient intelligence to know how to make use of it. Now it is my turn to give you an example: "Look at that ———; he is ——— tall.'"

"I must look at something," said Mary, "and all things are nouns, so it must be a noun; but I can find out more than that, mamma, for you say *he* in the last part of the sentence; so *he* must be the pronoun for the unknown noun, and that shows that he is an animal of the masculine gender; and I dare say it is either man or boy, because you do not call a common animal *he*."

"You are guessing the word again, Mary."

"I do not know how it is, mamma,—I always begin or finish by trying to guess the word."

"It may be very well for you," said mother, "to *begin* by thinking of the several words which might supply the blank, which would make sense; and when you have done this, and find that all these are of the same kind, you can then have no difficulty in ascertaining the part of speech which is wanting."

"But," said Mary, "it is much more difficult to think of a great many unknown words than of one single one; and I like thinking and talking of single individual things best."

"Because," continued her mother, "to think of a single individual thing requires less pains-taking; but when you have exerted yourself, and by intelligence and thought have discovered the part of speech, do you not feel a higher degree of pleasure than that of merely guessing right?"

"Oh yes, it is quite another sort of pleasure to get over a difficulty."

"It is therefore well worth while to make an exertion in order to do what gives such a superior and rational pleasure: any goose may guess, but he will seldom guess right; it is people of sense and information alone who can discover."

"Well, mamma, now I am going to exert myself to discover the last unknown part of speech in your phrase 'he is —— tall,'—something that comes before the adjective tall—no!" said she, interrupting herself, "it is not *something*, for that would be a noun; it must be a much more insignificant word, like *very*, or *rather*, or *extremely*; in short, it is an adverb, which gives force to the adjective."

"Very well," said her mother, "the complete phrase is, 'Look at that *man*—he is *very* tall.' Now, Mary, we have done enough of this to-day."

"Oh no," replied Mary, "it is so amusing, pray let us go through all the parts of speech."

"We may continue it to-morrow, if you please," answered her mother: "but if we went farther to-day, I should be afraid that you would grow tired of thinking, and would return to guessing."

PARSING, PART II

"I AM going to give you a very difficult example to-day, Mary," said her mother; "but you know the greater the pains required, the greater will be the pleasure if you succeed: '——— children stood ———, and then went ——— stairs.'"

"Three unknown words in one sentence!" exclaimed Mary. "The first word," continued she, "must be an adjective describing the sort of children."

"It might be an adjective, it is true," replied her mother, "such as pretty, good, or naughty children; but there is another part of speech which more commonly precedes a noun, especially at the beginning of a sentence."

"What can that be?" asked Mary; then, after a little, she added, "Oh yes! now I recollect, an article comes before a noun. Now which of the articles is it?—it is not the article *a*, for that cannot be placed before the plural noun children; nor can it be *an*, because the word children does not begin with a vowel; besides, *an* is a singular article as well as *a*, so it must be the definite article *the;* and the best of it is, mamma, that you must guess the word, as there is but one definite article."

"But you have not finished yet."

"Well, then," resumed Mary, " 'The children stood ——.' Stood is a verb, and the unknown word must be an adverb; but I should like to make out whether the adverb shows the manner, or place, or time of the verb—in short, mamma, in which of my drawers of adverbs I am to look for it. 'The children stood *still;'*—no!" continued she, "I don't think it is *still,* for children seldom stand still; besides they could not stand still, for they went somewhere; and yet, I think it means their manner of standing—I don't want to guess the exact word, you know, but yet I rather think," said she, "that they stood up."

Her mamma smiled, which confirmed her suspicion.

"Now then," continued Mary, "we come to the last word, and that is easy enough: it must be a preposition; for it shows the connection between the children and the stairs, and they could have no other connection with the stairs than going *up* them: unless," added she, laughing, "they went *down* stairs; but I think the sentence is this, 'The children stood *up,* and then went *up* stairs.' But how is this, mamma, here are two *ups* in the sentence, and yet they are different parts of speech?"

"You know, Mary, that sometimes happens. When you say the children stood up, the word means the manner in which the children stood, and is therefore an adverb; but when you say that they went *up* stairs, the word shows the relation between the two nouns *children* and *stairs*, and is consequently a preposition."

"Oh, mamma, I have thought of a sentence for you, but I must write it down;" and she took a pen and wrote as follows: "——! come ——, and look out of the window —— you will see a strange sight."

"You have helped me on with the first word prodigiously, Mary," said her mother; "it can be nothing but an interjection, since there is a note of admiration after it; and as there is a strange sight to be seen from the window, no doubt it is an interjection of surprise or wonder; as, oh! ah! Then, after the verb, the unknown word must be either an adverb or a conjunction."

"It can't be a conjunction," said Mary; "because there is a conjunction just after, come —— *and* look.' "

"True," replied her mother; "it is, then, an adverb."

"But, mamma, can you tell whether the adverb relates to place, or time, or number, or what?"

"I should think it related to place, but I cannot be certain; for though it is probably come *here*, or come *near*, it may be come *now*, or come *presently*; and the two last, you know, relate to time."

"Yes, yes—*here* is the word," said Mary.

"Well, then, the last word must be a conjunction," resumed her mother; "for it unites the two parts of the sentence, and I suppose it is *and* —'Oh! come here and look out of the window, and you will see a strange sight.' Now, Mary, I advise you to go into the garden, and see what strange sights are seen there, for you have had enough grammar for to-day."

LESSON XVIII

PARSING, PART III

THE next morning her mother told Mary that she believed they had gone through all the parts of speech in this mode of parsing; but, as she seemed to like it, she would give her another example: "Is that cake —— me? I should be glad if it were —— I am very hungry."

"The first unknown word must be a preposition," said Mary; "because it shows the relation between the *cake* and the pronoun *me*; and the last is a conjunction, because it joins the two sentences."

"Now, Mary, I give you leave to guess the two individual words."

"The first word must be *for*," said Mary; " 'Is that cake *for* me?' " Then, with a look of surprise, she added, "The last word is *for*, too: here are two more words like the two *ups*, mamma—both the same, and yet being different parts of speech!"

"That," replied her mother, "you know, happens not unfrequently, especially with adverbs, prepositions, and conjunctions. You may always distinguish the conjunction *for* from the adverb, by changing it into another conjunction—*because*, and observing whether it makes sense. You may say, *because* I am very hungry, instead of *for* I am very hungry. But you would not say, is this cake *because* me?"

"No, indeed!" said Mary, laughing, "that would be nonsense: so then, when *for* can be changed for another conjunction, it shows that it is a conjunction; and when it cannot, it shows that it is a preposition. But pray, mamma, tell me some more words which are the same, and yet belong to different parts of speech."

Her mother gave her the following example:— "Sophy came *in* to read, and looked *in* the drawer for her book."

"The first *in* is an adverb," said Mary, "added to the verb came, and the last *in* is a preposition, showing the connection between Sophy and drawer."

"Well," said her mother, "before you go *on* with your examples, pray put your gloves *on* your hands."

Mary smiled, and began drawing on her gloves; and while she was thus employed, she said, "Mamma, I believe I am to explain, instead of giving an example. The first *on* is an adverb, after the verb go; and the last *on* is a preposition showing the connection between my hands and my gloves; and a very close connection it is," said she, laughing; "for they fit so tightly, that it is very troublesome to get them either on or off."

Mary then asked her mamma for some words which belonged to more than two different parts of speech; but she answered, "That will be too difficult for you, my dear; you must wait with patience, and at some future time, when you are a little older, we may resume the subject. But before I conclude, I must ask you whether you have observed how every other part of speech relates to a noun?"

"Oh yes," said Mary, "the noun is the grand part of speech; all the others belong to it in some way or other, and could do nothing without it."

"Well then, try to tell me how the several parts of speech are connected with a noun. Begin with the adjective."

"The adjective," said Mary, "teaches you the distinguishing qualities of a noun."

"And the pronoun?" rejoined her mother.

"It stands in the place of a noun, so it is more nearly related to it than any of the other parts of speech are."

"And yet," said her mother, "though they are such near relations they never meet, for the one taking the place of the other, they are never wanted together. Now for the verb?"

"The verb tells you what the noun does."

"And the adverb?"

"Shows where, and when, and how the noun does the verb."

"And the preposition?"

"Points out the connection between two nouns."

"Then the articles?"

"Are placed before nouns, to show whether they are definite or indefinite."

"And the conjunction?"

"Joins words and sentences together."

"Lastly, the interjection?"

"Oh!" replied Mary, "the interjection makes the noun cry out for joy, or grief, or astonishment; as, oh! alas! etc."

"Extremely well," said her mother. "If you reflect a little you will find that in every sentence, however short, there is a noun, either said, or understood, or represented by a pronoun. When you speak, you must speak about somebody or something; you may talk about the qualities, the actions, or the manners of the noun, but the noun itself cannot be omitted, as it is essentially necessary to the discourse, though the other parts of speech are not so."

LESSONS I TO XVIII

QUESTIONS AND ANSWERS

NOUNS

Q. What is a noun?

A. It is a name.

Q. Of what is it the name?

A. It is the name of a person, place, or thing.

Q. Give examples.

A. John is a noun, because it is the name of a person. School-room is a noun, because it is the name of a place. Table is a noun, because it is the name of a thing.

Q. Are all animals, vegetables, and minerals nouns?

A. Yes, because they are all names.

Q. Give examples of each class.

A. First, Animals:—Dog, horse, lion, whale, lobster, crow, lark, worm, snake.

Secondly, Vegetables:—Tree, cabbage, rose, thistle, grass, fruit.

Thirdly, Minerals:—Earth, stones, coals, iron, silver.

Q. How do we discern these nouns?

A. By our five senses, and by our understanding.

Q. Give examples.

A. Apple is a noun, which I can see, feel, and taste. Wind is a noun; I can both feel and hear. Lightning is a noun; I can see. Water is a noun, which I can see, feel and taste.

Q. Are there any nouns which we cannot discover by the senses?

A. Yes, those which belong to the mind.

Q. Give examples.

A. Virtue, happiness, friendship, anger, sorrow, fear.

Q. How do we form an idea of things?

A. By our understanding alone, which makes us comprehend their meaning.

Q. Do we not feel sorrow, fear, love, etc.?

A. Not by our bodily senses, but we feel them by the sensations of the mind.

Q. Is every thing that exists a noun?

A. Yes, every thing, whether it relates to body or mind.

ADJECTIVES

Q. What is an adjective?

A. It is a word added to a noun.

Q. Of what use are adjectives?

A. They describe the qualities of nouns.

Q. Give examples.

A. A *black* horse, a *large* field, a *good* child.

Q. Have adjectives any other use?

A. By describing the qualities of nouns, they distinguish those of the same kind from one another.

Q. Give examples.

A. They distinguish a *black* horse from a *bay* horse, a *large* field from a *small* field, a *good* child from a *naughty* child.

Q. How many degrees of comparison have adjectives?

A. Three: the *Positive*, the *Comparative*, and the *Superlative*.

Q. What is the positive?

A. It affirms that a noun has such a quality.

Q. Give examples.

A. A *pretty* toy, a *tall* man.

Q. What is the comparative?

A. It compares two things together, to find out which has more and which less of the same quality.

Q. Give examples.

A. That toy is *prettier* than the other toy. John is *taller* than Tom.

Q. What is the superlative?

A. It is when a noun has more of the quality mentioned than other nouns with which it is compared.

Q. Give examples.

A. That toy is the *prettiest* of the three; John is the *tallest* of all.

Q. What is the termination of the comparative degree?

A. *Er*, as small*er*, bigg*er*, near*er*.

Q. What is the termination of the superlative degree?

A. *Est*, as small*est*, bigg*est*, near*est*.

ARTICLES

Q. What is an article?

A. It is a word placed before nouns to point them out.

Q. How many articles are there?

A. Two: *A* and *The*.

Q. What difference is there between these two articles?

A. *A* is the indefinite article; *The*, the definite article.

Q. What is the meaning of indefinite?

A. It speaks of the noun generally, without defining any particular one.

Q. Give examples.

A. *A* man, *a* house, *a* coat.

Q. What is the meaning of the definite article?

A. It defines or points out one particular noun, as *the* man I spoke to; *the* house I live in; *the* coat I wear.

Q. Can the article *a* be used before nouns either singular or plural?

A. No; before nouns singular only. You cannot say *a* coats, *a* tables.

Q. Can the article *the* be used before nouns of either number?

A. Yes; you may say *the* house, *the* houses; *the* dog, *the* dogs.

Q. Is there any change made in the indefinite article?

A. Yes, when *a* stands before a noun which begins with a vowel it is changed into *an*.

Q. Which are the vowels?

A. A, e, i, o, u, and y.

Q. Give examples in which *a* is changed into *an*.

A. *An* oyster, *an* ape.

Q. Is there any other case in which *an* must be used instead of *a?*

A. Yes; when *a* stands before a noun beginning with an *h* which is not aspirated.

Q. Give an example.

A. *An* honour, *an* hour.

Q. Does the definite article never change?

A. No: because *the* stands as well before a vowel as before a consonant, and before an *h*, whether aspirated or not.

Q. Give examples.

A. The apple, the table, the hour, the height.

Q. Can articles be placed before any other words besides nouns?

A Yes, they may be placed before an adjective when it is followed by a noun.

Q. Give examples.

A. *A* good man, *the* tall tree.

VERBS

Q. What is the meaning of a verb?

A. It signifies *to be, to do,* or *to suffer.*

Q. What is the meaning of a verb which signifies *to do?*

A. It is an action done by somebody or something.

Q. Give an example.

A. I *talk*, he *walks*, they *read*, we *hope*, she *expects*, it *falls*.

Q. Are *to hope* and *to expect*, actions?

A. Yes, they are actions of the mind.

Q. What is the meaning of a verb which signifies *to be* or *to suffer?*

A. It means a state of existence.

Q. Give me some examples.

A. To *be happy*, to *be sorry*, to *be tired*, to *be ill*.

Q. How many kinds of verbs are there?

A. Three; the active, the passive, and the neuter.

Q. What is an active verb?

A. It's doing something, to some person or thing.

Q. Give examples.

A. I *shut* the door, he *whips* the horse, she *stirs* the fire.

Q. What is the agent of a verb?

A. It is the person or thing which does the action.

Q. What is the object of a verb?

A. It is the person or thing acted upon by the agent.

Q. Give an example.

A. John *saddles* the pony.

Q. Which is the agent, and which the object?

A. *John* is the *agent* who performs the action of saddling the pony; the *pony* is the *object* acted upon by the agent.

Q. What is a *transitive* verb?

A. It is another name for a verb active, showing that the action passes over from the agent to the object.

Q. What is an intransitive verb?

A. It is one which does not pass over to an object.

Q. What is a passive verb?

A. A verb which signifies being acted upon.

Q. Give an example.

A. The mouse is caught.

Q. Is mouse the agent, or the object?

A. Mouse is the object caught.

Q. Which is the agent?

A. It is not named.

Q. Give an example of a passive verb in which the agent is named.

A. The *mouse* is caught by the *cat*.

Q. Which is the agent?

A. The cat which catches the mouse.

Q. Which is the object?

A. The mouse is the object caught.

Q. What difference is there between an active and a passive verb?

A. In an active verb the action is performed on an object; in a passive verb the action is received by an object.

Q. Give an example of an active verb.

A. Harry strokes the dog.

Q. Give an example of a passive verb.

A. The dog is stroked by Harry.

Q. Is there an agent and an object in all active verbs?

A. Yes, there must be an agent to act, and an object to be acted upon.

Q. What is a neuter verb?

A. It is an action performed independently of any object.

Q. Give examples.

A. Tom *jumps*, John *swims*, the broom *sweeps*, it *scratches*.

Q. Is there no object in the neuter verb?

A. No.

Q. And why?

A. Because in a neuter verb you do not act on any object.

Q. What is an impersonal verb?

A. It is a verb which has only the third person *it;* as, it rains, it thunders, etc.

ADVERBS

Q. What is an adverb?

A. It is a word added to a verb.

Q. What are the uses of adverbs?

A. They show something relative to the verb to which they are added.

Q. What does the first class of adverbs show?

A. It shows the *manner* in which the verb is done.

Q. Give an example.

A. Tom writes *badly.*

Q. What does the second class show?

A. It *points* out the place in which the verb is done.

Q. Give examples.

A. I walked *here*, John slept *there.*

Q. Do not adverbs sometimes name the place?

A. No; if they named it they would be nouns, not adverbs.

Q. What does the third class of adverbs show?

A. It points out the *time* of doing the verb.

Q. Give examples.

A. I will go *directly*; he is coming *presently*. I *never* saw her.

Q. Do adverbs ever name the time?

A. No, they only point it out; names are always nouns.

Q. What does the fourth class of adverbs show?

A. It points out the *number* of times the verb is done.

Q. Give examples.

A. I spoke *once*, he laughed *twice*, Susan coughed *thrice*.

Q. To what does the fifth class of adverbs relate?

A. To the *quantity* of the verb.

Q. Give examples.

A. I have talked *much*, my brother sneezed *often*, Sophy cried a *little*.

Q. What does the sixth class of adverbs do?

A. It asks questions.

Q. Give examples.

A. *How* did you come? *When* will you eat?

Q. What does the seventh class of adverbs do?

A. It answers questions.

Q. Give examples.

A. *No*, certainly; *yes*, willingly.

Q. Have adverbs ever degrees of comparison?

A. Some adverbs have.

Q. Give examples.

A. Well, *better*, *best*, much, *more, most*.

Q. Are adverbs ever joined to other words, so as to make but one word?

A. Yes.

Q. Give examplcs.

A. They are sometimes joined to verbs; as *overthrow, overdone*. Sometimes to nouns, as *underhand, overhead*.

PREPOSITIONS

Q. What is a preposition?

A. It is a word which serves to connect nouns or other words, and shows their relation to each other.

Q. Give examples.

A. Put some coals *on* the fire; throw the paper *into* the fire; place the screen *before* the fire, and the chair *near* the fire.

Q. Explain these examples.

A. The preposition *on* shows the relation between the nouns coals and fire; the preposition *into*, the relation between the paper and the fire; the preposition *before*, the connection between the screen and the fire; the preposition *near*, the relation between the chair and the fire.

A. Do prepositions show the relation between pronouns as well as nouns?

A. Yes.

Q. Give examples.

A. Will *you* come *to me? They* went away *from us.*

Q. Does a preposition ever become an adverb?

A. Yes.

Q. Give an example.

A. Put some plates *on* the table; go *on*, there are not enough yet.

Q. Explain the example.

A. The first *on* is a preposition, because it shows the relation between plates and table. The last *on* is an adverb, because it is added to the verb *go*.

Q. Are prepositions ever joined to other words, so as to make a compound word?

A. Yes; they are sometimes joined to nouns, and sometimes to verbs.

Q. Give examples.

A. In the words *underwrite, overtake, upset,* they are joined to verbs. In *overboard, underground,* they are joined to nouns.

CONJUNCTIONS

Q. What is a conjunction?

A. A conjunction connects words and sentences together.

Q. Give examples.

A. Come *and* read. Put on your hat, *if* you go out.

Q. What is a *copulative* conjunction?

A. It connects the actions or things spoken of, as well as the words.

Q. Give examples.

A. Will you read *and* write? You are *as* tall *as* I am.

Q. What are *disjunctive* conjunctions?

A. They join the words, but disjoin the action or things spoken of.

Q. Give examples.

A. Will you *neither* read *nor* write? I will give you an apple *or* a pear.

INTERJECTION

Q. What is an interjection?

A. It is a cry or exclamation, expressing some emotion of the mind, either admiration, surprise, terror, grief, or weariness.

Q. Give examples.

A. Oh! ah! alas! heigh-ho! ah, well-a-day!

Q. What is the sign of the interjection?

A. A note of admiration which follows it.

LESSON XIX

NOUNS—NUMBER

MARY having passed some months without learning any grammar, her mother asked her one day whether she would not like to know more of the different parts of speech; thinking that, as she was now eight years old, she was capable of proceeding further in the study. Mary was very willing to do so: she had no longer any dislike to grammar; and if she thought it a little tiresome sometimes, she remembered that the story at the end used to make up for all.

"You mean to go on with the stories, too, mamma?" said she, smiling. Her mother consented; but on condition that she would make them useful as parsing exercises.

"I do not think it necessary," said she, "to teach you any thing more on articles, adjectives, adverbs, conjunctions, prepositions, or interjections. What you have learnt of them is sufficient for a child of your age; but there is a great deal more to be said on nouns, pronouns, and verbs." Mary was glad of that; for those were the parts of speech she liked the best.

"We will begin with the nouns or substantives,"

143

said her mother. "A noun, you recollect, is the name of any thing; and you must try to remember that it is but the name, for beginners are very apt to suppose that it means the thing itself; but if you imprint it on your memory that *noun* is only the Latin for *name*, you will avoid this error. I then explained to you that nouns were the names of different sorts of things, such as *persons, places*, and *inanimate objects*, all of which were discerned by our senses; but I did not make you acquainted with a class of nouns the objects of which cannot be perceived by the senses."

"Those must be curious nouns," observed Mary, "which can neither be seen, heard, or discovered by any sense! How is it possible to find them out?"

"If I did not make you acquainted with them sooner," replied her mother, "it was because I thought them too difficult for a beginner; but now that you have made some little progress in grammar, I think that you will be able to comprehend these strange nouns. They are discerned by the understanding alone: *virtue, honesty, greatness, goodness*, and *wickedness* are of this description."

"Well!" exclaimed Mary. "I never should have supposed these words to have been nouns: surely they are not the names of things?"

"Not of bodily things, which we can see, or feel, or perceive by any of our senses; but they are the *names* of things which we can understand the meaning of. If I say that *happiness* is the reward of a good conscience, you understand what I mean by happiness?"

144

"Oh yes," replied Mary; "it is something that I like very much—that everybody likes. Happiness gives us joy, pleasure, and all sorts of good things."

"And what is *goodness?*" inquired her mother.

"*Goodness,*" said Mary, "is doing every thing right; and *greatness* is something very large."

"Greatness," observed her mother, "may relate, not to the body, but to the mind. Pope was a very great poet, though he was a very little man."

"But, mamma, you say that we cannot perceive these nouns by our senses; yet I am sure that I *feel happiness,* and *kindness,* and *gratitude,* and all those difficult nouns which belong to the mind."

"What you feel," said her mother, "are not the outward feelings of touch, but the inward feelings of the mind; for we cannot discern such nouns by any of our external senses, as we do table and chairs, or thunder and lightning."

"Oh no! certainly," said Mary, "it is quite a different feeling."

"Nouns are divided into two sorts, proper and common. A noun proper is the name of any individual person, place, or thing."

Mary inquired what an individual meant?

"It means," said her mother, "any one particular thing. You are an individual, and your name *Mary* is a noun *proper;* because it distinguishes you from other children: but when I call you *child,* that is a noun

145

common; because it belongs to all other children as well as to you."

"But *Mary* does not belong to me only, mamma; for we know Mary Hunter, and Mary Banks, and a great many other Marys."

"Several persons may have the same name; but still it is the individual name of each; it does not belong to all women and children. If I say *children*, it is a noun *common*, because it belongs to the whole class of children. If I say *boy*, it is a noun *common* to all boys, and *girl* is a noun *common* to all girls; but if I say *John*, or *Harriet*, those are nouns *proper*, that is, belonging to particular individuals."

"Oh yes, I understand the difference; church is a noun common to all churches; but St. Paul's is a noun proper to that church only."

"Town," said her mother, "is a noun common to all cities; but London, York, and Bristol, are nouns proper to those towns."

"And dog, mamma, is common to all dogs; but Alpin and Carlo are the proper names of our two dogs."

The next thing to be considered, with regard to nouns, her mother told her, was their number.

"What an immense number there must be!" exclaimed Mary; "for the name of every thing in the whole world, you know, is a noun."

"The meaning of number in grammar," her mother said, "is much more simple: it consists only of two, the *singular* and the *plural*. The singular means one—a single thing; and the plural means more than one."

"Oh yes, I know that," said Mary; "but does not singular also mean something very odd or strange? Suppose we were to see a very funny-looking carriage passing by, you would say, 'Look, what a singular carriage that is!'"

"It is true," replied her mother, "that singular is often used in that sense; but the original meaning is the same. You call the carriage singular, because there is no other like it; if so, the carriage is single or alone of its kind, and is therefore of the singular number."

"Ah! so it is. Well, that is very singular," said Mary, laughing; "but, mamma, you never say that a common coach or carriage, that is not singular, is plural: do you?"

"No," replied her mother; "the word plural is never used in any other sense than *more than one.*"

"So, then," said Mary, "a singular carriage, or a singular thing, does not so much mean that it is something very comical, as that it is singular from having nothing else like it, and standing alone."

"That, no doubt, was the original meaning of the word singular; but it is so commonly used to express extraordinary things, that the idea of strange and wonderful became attached to it; and that of being alone or single of its kind was generally forgotten. What is your idea of the word *odd*, Mary?"

"Something very droll that makes one laugh."

"Does an odd glove make you laugh?"

"Oh dear, no!" exclaimed Mary. "It makes me more inclined to cry; for you know that you are displeased with me when I have lost one of my gloves, and have only an odd one; but that *odd* is quite another word from the odd that makes you laugh; at least, it has another meaning."

"I believe, my dear, that it is not only the same word; but that, like *singular*, it had originally the same meaning. An odd glove means that it has no fellow, so that it is alone or singular; and when you say an odd person, who makes you laugh, or stare with wonder, the original meaning was, a man so unlike others, that he was alone or singular. Now for the plural number."

"The plural," said Mary, "I know, means a great many things."

"Not always a great many, for two is plural as well as a thousand; the plural, therefore, speaks of any number more than one. It is usually formed by adding the letter *s* to the singular; thus, the plural of dog is dogs."

"Oh yes," said Mary; "and the plural of boy, boys; girl, girls; and of child, childs—oh no; that is not right," cried she, interrupting herself, "the plural of child is children."

"Very true; though the plural is most commonly formed by the addition of an *s*, there are many exceptions to this rule, of which child and children affords one example; but there are a variety of others. Tell me what is the plural of church?"

148

"It is churches," replied Mary.

"Then you see that you add *es* to church to make it plural; you could not say churchs, you would not know how to pronounce it. The same is the case with the words brush, sash, box, kiss, and almost all nouns that end in *s*, double *s*, and *ch* pronounced soft, *sh*, and *x*."

"Yes," replied Mary; "the plural of brush is brush*es*; of kiss, kiss*es*; of sash, sash*es*; of box, box*es*. But what do you mean by *ch* pronounced soft?"

"As it is pronounced in the word church. In the word monarch, it is said to be pronounced hard, and then only *s* is added to render its plural. Now tell me what are the plurals of the words loaf, wife, and calf?"

"Loaves, wives, and calves," replied Mary; "in those words, therefore, *ves* is added."

Her mother then told her, that in almost all nouns ending either in *f*, as loaf, or in *fe*, as wife, the *f* or the *fe* must be taken away and the *ves* be put in its place to form the plural.

Mary thought of an example. "The plural of half," said she, "is halves; of life, lives; of knife, knives: oh! I shall not forget that."

Her mother then bid her observe, that nouns ending in y, with a consonant before the *y*, form the plural in *ies*; as, fly, flies; quantity, quantities.

Mary thought that there was no end to the variations in changing from singular to plural, and that it was rather puzzling. But her mother said, that there were some nouns which did not change at all, and which were, perhaps, still more perplexing; as *sheep*, for instance. "Can you tell me whether the word sheep is singular or plural?"

"No, indeed; I cannot, unless you say whether you are speaking of one sheep or of several."

"That is because sheep is both singular and plural. You are, therefore, obliged to point out the number by saying, 'There is a sheep,' or, 'There are some sheep.' When you say *a* sheep, I know it is singular, because the article *a* is never put before plural nouns. But if you say *the* sheep, it would be impossible to know whether you meant one or many; because the article *the* may be placed before either singular or plural nouns."

"Then how can you find it out, mamma?"

"You may either mention the number; or, if you are talking of what the sheep are doing, the verb will point out the number; as, the sheep *is* feeding; or the sheep *are* feeding."

"That is," said Mary, "the verb will point out whether the number is singular or plural, but not the precise number if it is plural."

"Certainly not; you must remember that when we talk of number in grammar, we mean only the singular and the plural."

"But, mamma, if I said a flock of sheep, what would that be? for there is only one flock, and a great number of sheep, so that the flock is singular and the sheep are plural."

150

"Very true: but which of the two are you talking of?"

"Of both together," replied Mary; "if I said a flock by itself, it would be singular: but if I say a flock of sheep, it seems to be both singular and plural at once."

"That cannot be," said her mother; "a flock of sheep is of the singular number; it is the *flock* you are speaking of, the sheep are only mentioned as being the animals of which the flock is composed." Mary did not seem quite satisfied with this explanation; she did not think it fair towards the sheep. Then her mother added, that nouns of this description were distinguished by the name of nouns of multitude, showing that though they are of the singular number, they consist of a great many individuals. That a crowd, a congregation, an assembly, were all nouns of multitude.

"Let me think of some," said Mary; "there is a *herd* of cattle as well as a *flock* of sheep, and a *drove* of pigs, and then a *swarm* of bees. *Your* nouns of multitude were all made up of people, mamma, and *mine* are made up of common animals or insects; but are there nouns of multitude for things also?"

"What do you think of a *forest* of trees, Mary, a *ton* of coals, a *load* of gravel, or a *nosegay* of flowers?"

Her mother then told her that there were some nouns that were of the plural number only; as, scissors, bellows, snuffers, tongs, and many others.

"I think I can guess why they are of the plural number, mamma. Scissors, you know, are made of two blades that cut, and two handles, so it is a sort of double instrument, and that must be the reason why it is called plural; and bellows, and tongs, and snuffers, are all made of two halves also."

Her mother thought it very possible that she might be right in her conjecture. She then wrote down some few nouns, which vary in the singular and the plural numbers in a very irregular manner; as follows:—

Goose,	Geese.
Penny,	Pence.
Tooth,	Teeth.
Foot,	Feet.
Mouse,	Mice.
Man,	Men.
Woman,	Women.
Child,	Children.
Brother,	Brothers, or Brethren.

Mary having now learnt the meaning of a noun proper and a noun common, and also the difference between the singular and the plural number, her mother said it was as much as she could well remember at once. She would, therefore, reserve what she had farther to say on nouns till the next lesson.

LESSON XX

NOUNS—GENDER

MARY's mother told her that she would now explain to her the *genders* of nouns: that there were three genders, the *masculine*, the *feminine*, and the *neuter*.

"These are all new words, mamma," said Mary; "and I do not understand one of them."

Her mother said that every thing of the *he* kind was masculine, therefore a man, a bull, a lion, a drake, were all of the masculine gender; and that every thing of the *she* kind was feminine, therefore a woman, a cow, a lioness, a duck, were of the feminine gender.

"And is there no gender that means young creatures, like little boys and girls, and chickens and ducklings?" inquired Mary.

"No: for they are all either of the masculine or the feminine gender."

"Oh yes; boys and girls grow up to be men and women," said Mary; "and I suppose the little ducklings will grow up into ducks and drakes."

"Yes; and thus all animals are of the masculine or the feminine gender."

"But, then, mamma, what is there left to belong to the neuter gender?"

"The word neuter signifies neither, therefore neuter gender means neither gender."

"So every thing which is neither masculine nor feminine must belong to the neuter gender?"

"Every thing that is not an animal; and there are a tolerable number, Mary, for that gender."

"Do you mean things and places; such as a house, a table, a field?"

"Yes, and every inanimate thing that can be put upon the table, and that is in the house, and that grows in the field; for grass, and trees, and all vegetables are of the neuter gender."

"And minerals, too," said Mary, "I suppose; earth, and coals, and stones; and then the metals, mamma, gold and silver, and lead and iron, and I know not how many others."

"Nor I, Mary; it would be impossible to enumerate all the nouns of the neuter gender; and yet they may all be comprised in one little sentence; every thing excepting animals."

"Why, then, after all," said Mary, "I dare say that there are more nouns of the neuter gender than there are of the masculine and feminine genders."

"I believe that would be difficult to determine; for no one knows what number of animals there are in the world, or of vegetables and minerals either."

"I thought, mamma, learned men knew all those things."

"They know a great deal more than we do, my dear: but it is God alone who knows all that he has made; and the more we learn of his works the better; for the more we shall know how good, and great, and wise he is."

Mary was awed by the solemnity of her mother's manner; and though she felt the force of her words, she did not venture to make any remark; and her mother went on with her lesson, and asked her if she knew what pronoun was used for the masculine gender?

"I say, *he* or *him*, for a man, mamma; and *she* and *her*, for a woman: but what is the pronoun for the neuter gender?"

"Do not you recollect? in speaking of this table, for instance."

"I should say, it is too heavy for me to move. Yes, *it* is the pronoun for the neuter gender. I remember, I found *it* out myself."

"The plural pronouns, they, them, their, those, will suit all the genders equally well; for you may say, 'Do not eat *those* apples, *they* are sour; *their* seeds are bitter; throw *them* away;' and you may also say, 'Look at *those* men and women, *they* are very busy; *their* work is hard, I should like to help *them*.' "

"But, mamma, I heard you say the other day, when you were looking at that great ship in the river, how beautifully *she* sails! and yet a ship is not an animal, and is not alive, though it sails."

"Very true, Mary, an animal does not sail; it swims and moves itself in the water; while a ship sails, because the wind blows against its sails, and makes it go on."

"Then, why did you call the ship *she*, as if it were a living animal of the feminine gender?"

"It is sometimes permitted when we speak of any thing very grand, or very beautiful, to personify it; that is, to pretend, or (as you would say) make believe, that it is a person. Thus, we often call the sun *he*, and say, 'The sun is shining in all *his* glory; *he* gives us light and heat;' and when we personify the moon, we use the feminine gender, and say, '*She* shines upon us with *her* soft silvery light.'"

"I know," said Mary, "that the gardener calls his spade *he*; for I heard him say one day, *he* is a famous spade; then the coachman calls his whip *he*, too; but I am sure that cannot be because the spade and the whip are grand or beautiful."

"No; it is an improper manner of speaking, not uncommon amongst ignorant people. They think they bestow a mark of regard on any thing they are proud of or fond of, by speaking of it as they would do of a person. This is so common among the peasantry in some parts of the country, that they call almost every thing *he* and *she*. I recollect last summer a poor woman who had broken her arm saying, *she* had hurt her shocking bad all the night: and as I had desired a woman to sit up with her, I concluded (till the matter was explained), that it was the nurse who had hurt her, and not the arm."

"Well," said Mary, "I do not personify any thing but

my doll, and I am sure she has a right to it, she looks so pretty, and so much as if she was alive."

"Well, you may go and play with her now," said her mother; "for the lesson is finished, and to-morrow I intend to treat you with a story."

A STORY

BLIND TOMMY

HARRY VILLARS was walking one day with his parents, by the side of a river; the path was broad, and far enough from the water's edge to prevent any danger of his falling in. His mamma, therefore, gave him leave to run on before, to gather the cowslips which grew on the bank. Harry observed a little boy at some distance before him, who had collected a quantity of cowslips, and he called to his papa and mamma to beg them to hasten on, as he wanted to overtake the child in order to see the ball of cowslips, which he was tying up. They had nearly reached the boy at a turn of the river; but he, instead of following the winding path which continued alongside the water, walked straight on to the brink and fell in. Mr. and Mrs. Villars, and Harry ran to the spot, and saw the poor child struggling in the water; Mr. Villars instantly threw off his hat and coat and plunged in: but before he could reach the boy his screams of distress had ceased, he had sunk to the bottom, and nothing was to be seen but the scattered cowslips floating on the surface of the stream. Harry, whose cries had almost equalled those of the child before he sank, became still more terrified when he saw his father in the water. His mother tried to pacify him, by showing him how well his father could swim, and saying she hoped he would be able to save the child. "But he is drowned," sobbed Harry, "and papa will be drowned too." His papa hallooed out to him that there was no danger for himself; and that though the boy had sunk, he would soon rise again, and then he would try to catch hold of him. A few moments afterwards the child was seen rising to the surface; but the current of the stream had carried him to some distance and was bearing him still farther off from the spot where Mr. Villars was swimming: the instant Mr. Villars perceived him, he swam after him so fast, that he soon overtook him, seized hold of him by the hair, and dragged him ashore. Mrs. Villars and Harry, who had followed along the bank of the river, reached the spot just as he was brought to land. The poor boy appeared quite lifeless, and Mr. Villars himself, dripping with wet, carried him in his arms to a neighbouring cottage. He was there undressed and put into a warm bed: and in a short time, to the great joy of all, he showed signs of returning animation, and soon after opened his eyes; but they were shocked to see them without any expression, and looking quite dead, though the rest of his body was restored to life. "Alack a day!" exclaimed the dame of the cottage, "if this is not poor blind Tommy! Run, Jack (said she to her son), and fetch his mother." The accident was now accounted for; poor Tommy had walked into the river, not from heedlessness, but because he could not see.

When the mother arrived she was sadly distressed at the state in which she found her son. But the instant he heard her voice, he called to her; and clasping his arms round her neck, said, "Oh, dear mother! I thought I should never kiss you again; I thought I was quite drowned." The poor woman reproached herself for letting her blind boy go out alone; she said that she wished to keep him more at home, under her own eye; but that he was so fond of rambling about in the open air, that she could not find in her heart to refuse him; especially as he was very careful in general, and had never met with a serious accident before.

"I will never do so any more," cried poor little Tommy, as if he had committed a fault; "I was so busy with my cowslips, that I did not find out I had lost the path till I fell into the water; and now all my sweet cowslips are lost!"

"But how could you see the cowslips without eyes?" said Harry.

"I did not see them," replied the boy, "I smelt them; and when I stooped to gather them, I felt them."

"Well, I don't think I could smell cowslips," said Harry, "if I shut my eyes; and so I should not know where to stoop down to gather them."

Tommy seemed too weak to talk any more: but his mother answered for him, and said, "You have eyes to see with, my little master; but my poor boy, who has none, is obliged to snuff about with his nose, like a dog, to find out things by their smell; so, at last, he has learnt to smell almost as well as a dog; and he can hear a deal better than those who see," continued she; "and when the pot is set to boil on the fire, he is on the watch, and comes to tell me the instant it begins to bubble, that I may take it off before it boils over."

Tommy was then left quiet; and Harry allowed to watch by the bedside, on condition that he should not speak to him. Mrs. Villars retired with the mother to the further end of the room, and asked her whether she would like her son to be placed at the Blind Institution.

"Ah! that is what I have been trying for many a year, ma'am," said the poor woman, "but never could get him in. At first, Tommy was very much against it himself, not liking to leave us; but now he is grown older, and finds what a trouble his blindness is to us all, he has made up his mind to it, if we could but get him elected."

"Then, after this accident," said Mrs. Villars, "he will, probably, grow more timid, and be glad to be settled in a place where he will feel perfectly secure."

She promised to endeavour to get him into the Institution; and whilst they were talking the matter over, in a low voice, Harry, who had been watching by the bedside came up, and whispered, "Mamma, he is gone to sleep." Mrs. Villars then took leave, being impatient to join her husband, who had left them as soon as he found the boy was safe, in order to get dry clothes. She assured the boy's mother that if she was careful his sleep should not be disturbed, he would, probably, be quite well when he awoke.

The next day Mrs. Villars went to the Blind Institution, and took Harry with her. He was much surprised to see so many blind people, and how cleverly they did what they were about. The women and little girls worked at their needle as neatly as if they could see, and sang whilst they were at work: and when they were tired of singing, one of the matrons read to them. The men and boys were busy making baskets, weaving mats and ropes, and a variety of works which Harry thought very amusing.

They afterwards went into the refectory, to see the blind people at dinner; and when Harry inquired what this and that dish was, they answered him readily before they had tasted: "This is boiled mutton, that is stewed potatoes; we know them by their smell."

As they were returning home, Harry could talk of nothing but the blind people; he observed that they felt, and smelt, and heard so much better than he could, that they hardly seemed to want eyes.

"That is true," replied his mother; "God Almighty, in his goodness, softens the affliction of blindness by rendering the other senses more acute by use."

"Then, mamma, after all," said Harry, "perhaps, Tommy is as happy as I am,—when he don't fall into the water!"

"Oh no!" replied she; "think what a pity it is that poor Tommy cannot see all the pretty things which delight your eyes. He cannot see the beautiful colours of the flowers that smell so sweet, nor the green branches of the trees under which he plays, nor the clear sky, nor the bright sunshine in his mother's eyes when she is pleased to see him good and happy."

"Oh, dear, no!" said Harry, "that is a sad thing, indeed;" and he looked at his mother with an expression of tenderness which brought the sunshine into her eyes at once.

Mrs. Villars interested herself so much to obtain an admission for poor Tommy, that at the next election he was chosen, and went to live in the Asylum. He was often visited by his mother, and, at least once a year, by Mrs. Villars and her son, who always brought him some token of their regard.

LESSON XXI

NOUNS—CASES

"I SHALL this morning teach you the cases of nouns, Mary," said her mother.

"Cases!" repeated Mary, "what can they be? not cases to keep nouns in, surely?"

"No," replied her mother; "the cases of nouns have quite another meaning; you know that the same word has sometimes more than one meaning."

"What! like the word singular, mamma, which sometimes mean one single thing, and sometimes a thing that is strange or odd?"

"Yes; have you never heard the word *case* used in any other sense than to keep things in?"

"Oh yes, mamma, I have just thought of another *case*. Do you remember when I was ill, and Dr. Berkeley came to see me: he said, 'Well, my little dear, let us hear your *case*;' and I stared, for I did not know what he meant, till he asked me whether I had a headache, or was thirsty, and a number of other questions, and so I suppose that he wanted to find out what was the matter with me."

"Yes; it was necessary that he should know in what state or condition your health was, in order to give you proper remedies; and *state* and *condition* signify *case*."

"I thought that state and condition meant something very dirty and ugly," said Mary, "for when I splash my frock in watering my garden, nurse says, 'Oh! what a condition you are in!' or, 'What a state your frock is in!'"

"State and condition mean *how* your frock is; it may be in a good state, as well as in a bad one; in a clean condition, as well as in a dirty one."

"Yes," said Mary; "when the doctor inquired so much about my health, it was in a bad state, not a good one; nurse says sometimes, 'Let me see if your frock is in a fit state for you to go into the drawing-room;' and then she does not mean dirty, but whether it is clean enough for the drawing-room."

"Well, then, Mary, if you understand what state and condition mean, I hope you will not find it difficult to understand the different cases of nouns, which means nothing more than their different state or condition."

"I dare say I shall not, mamma, when you explain them to me; but I cannot say that I do now."

"Nouns have three different cases," said her mother; "the *Nominative*, the *Possessive*, and the *Objective*."

Mary made a long face at these hard names.

"They are not so difficult as you imagine, my dear. If I say the dog barks, or the dog is tired, it means that the dog *does* something or *is* something; does it not?"

"Yes, certainly," replied Mary. "It means the dog *does* bark, or *is* tired."

"Dog is the noun, and the verb which follows shows you what the dog *does* or *is*."

"Yes," said Mary; "barks is a verb, and so is being tired."

"Well, then, *doing* something, or being something, is one state or condition of the noun 'dog;' and when the dog is *doing* something, as when the dog is running; or when the dog is *being* something, as when the dog is tired; *dog* is said to be in the *nominative* case."

"Then there is always a verb after the nominative case?" said Mary.

"Yes, in order to point out what the noun is doing or being."

"I wish," said Mary, "it was called the doing and being case; then I should understand and remember it much more easily than the hard word nominative."

"That is true," said her mother; "for nominative is a Latin word, which means simply to name the noun."

"Now let me find out some nominative cases," said Mary. "Sophy laughs; *Sophy* is the nominative case because she *does* something. He is hungry: *he* is the nominative case, because he *is* something. The nominative case seems quite easy now; the noun comes first, and the verb that follows tells you what the noun does."

"A pronoun may be nominative as well as a noun,

Mary; it is better, therefore, to say, the nominative comes first, instead of the noun comes first."

"Yes," replied Mary, "because nominative applies both to the noun and the pronoun equally well. *Sophy* is a nominative noun, and *he* a nominative pronoun: and what are the other cases mamma?"

"Let us return to the dog: suppose I were to speak about the dog's collar, or the dog's food, would that mean that the dog does something, or is something?"

"Oh no," said Mary; "it means that the dog has something that belongs to him. That is quite a different case."

"There! Mary," exclaimed her mother; "you have said the word *case* without thinking of it; but can you tell me what 'quite a different case' means?"

"No, indeed, mamma; I do not understand it enough to explain it."

"Then I must do it for you. It means that the state or condition of the dog is different in the one case from the other; that is, whether he *does* or *is* something, or whether he *has* something belonging to him. Well, then, since these cases are so different it is proper to call them by different names. The first, I have told you, is called the nominative case, and the second the *Possessive case*. Perhaps you can guess why it is so called?"

"I suppose because the dog possesses something; as, in the sentences, 'The dog's food,' 'The dog's collar:' the food is his; it belongs to him, and so does the collar too."

"You are quite right, my dear, but observe that it is not the food nor the collar of the dog that is in the possessive case, but only the dog itself."

"Oh yes, certainly," said Mary, "for the food and the collar possess nothing, it is the dog that possesses them. Now pray, mamma, let me try to find out some nouns in the possessive case. The child's doll, mamma's bonnet, Willy's hoop."

Her mother took a pen and wrote down the words Mary had just spoken; and Mary inquired why she put a comma before the *s* to all nouns in the possessive case. She replied, that if dogs were written without a comma before the *s*, it would mean several dogs instead of one dog.

"Oh yes; the dogs food would mean the food of a great many dogs; dogs would be of the plural number: you see," said Mary, smiling, "I don't forget about the plural number."

"But," said her mother, "in the plural number, it is also necessary to distinguish the possessive case from the other cases, by a comma; which is then placed *after* the *s* instead of *before* it; as, the dogs' food, with the comma after the *s*, means the food of several dogs."

"But, mamma, you do not pronounce the comma, you know; so, in speaking, how can you tell whether it is put before or after the noun, as the sound is the same?"

"You undoubtedly cannot, Mary; if the gamekeeper came in and talked about the dogs food, I should not know whether he meant the food of any particular dog, or that of all the dogs in the kennel; the words must be written to be distinguished."

"And is not this very puzzling, mamma?"

"No: I should probably be able to make out easily whether the gamekeeper was speaking about one or several dogs by the rest of his sentence. Besides, the difference may be distinguished by saying the food of the dog, or the food of the dogs, for the food of the *dog* or *dogs* is just as much in the possessive case as the dog's food."

And the collar *of the dog* must be so too," said Mary.

"Yes, a noun which indicates possession is in the possessive case."

That makes the meaning quite clear," said Mary; "but why, mamma, are there always two nouns in the possessive case? In the dog's collar, for instance, the noun dog is followed by the noun collar, instead of being followed by a verb, as in the nominative case."

"If you think a little, Mary, you will find it out yourself. What is the possessive case?"

"It is a noun that possesses something," answered Mary: "a man who possesses a gun, a horse, a house, or any thing whatever."

"And pray what part of speech is that any thing?"

"It must be a noun," said Mary, "for you know all the things in the whole world are nouns. Oh! now I understand it: the first noun possesses the thing, and the second noun is the thing it possesses; as, Sophy's doll, John's horse, Betty's broom. Sophy possesses the doll, John possesses the horse, and Betty the broom; so there *must* be two nouns in the possessive case."

"Whilst in the nominative case," observed her mother, "nothing is possessed, but something is done; therefore the noun is followed by the verb which shows what is done.

"But though there are always two nouns when the possessive case is used," continued she, "they are not both in the possessive case: finish the sentence, 'John's horse,' for instance, and say, 'John's horse trots fast.' John's is possessive; but is horse in the possessive case also?"

"No," said Mary; "John possesses the horse, but the horse possesses nothing, it only trots:—Oh! now I know what case horse is in; it is nominative, because it does something."

Her mother said she was right; and Mary, pleased by her success, went on to give an example of the two cases herself.

"If I say, 'Sophy's doll is very pretty,' Sophy is possessive, because she possesses the doll; but doll is nominative, because she *is* something, she is very pretty."

"You are quite right; and in these instances the first noun is in the possessive, and the last in the nominative case. We will finish now, Mary, and leave the objective case for the next lesson."

LESSON XXII

NOUNS—OBJECTIVE CASE

"To-day, Mary," said her mother, "we are to finish the cases of nouns."

"I shall not be sorry for that," replied Mary; "for I think they are the most difficult of all I have learnt yet."

"They certainly require a little thought and pains-taking; but you have only one more case to learn, the *Objective*. This case is so much connected with the verb active, that I wish you would tell me whether you recollect well the meaning of a verb active?"

"Oh yes," said Mary; "the active verb tells you what the noun does."

"That is not all, Mary."

"I don't know how it is, mamma," said Mary, rather impatiently; "I always forget that in an active verb the action must be done to somebody or to something."

"Yes," said her mother, "the action must pass over to an object; as, John beats the dog. It is however a very natural mistake, to think the action of doing something sufficient to make a verb active: but it is not so; for however great the action, it is a neuter verb, unless it passes over to an object. It is for this reason that the verb active is also called transitive, which means to pass over; thus showing that the action passes over from the agent to the object. When I say, 'John beats the dog,' the action passes over from John to the dog."

"Well, mamma, I don't think I shall forget it any more. A verb active must have an agent to act or do the verb, and *also* an object to be acted upon; as, 'The horse eats corn.'"

"Then, my dear, the corn, which is the object acted upon, is in the objective case."

"Is that all?" said Mary, surprised and pleased that the difficulty, which she had feared, was so easily overcome; "why, nothing can be more easy; do let me think of some examples. Sophy strokes the *cat*; the cat is the object stroked, and so cat is in the objective case."

"And *Sophy*, who strokes it," said her mother, "is nominative."

"Yes," replied Mary, "Sophy is the agent. So then in the objective case there must always be two nouns; one to be the agent, the other to be the object."

"There must always be two nouns when the objective case is used, it is true," said her mother; "but they are not both in the objective case; the agent is nominative, and the object is objective."

"Oh yes, Sophy is nominative, and cat is objective."

"And observe," said her mother, "the nominative noun comes before the verb, and the objective noun after the verb; thus Sophy comes before the verb stroke, and cat after it."

"But when you taught me the nominative case in the last lesson, mamma, you told me that it always came before the verb, but you said nothing about the objective case coming after the verb; I remember the example you gave was, 'The dog barks.'"

"I wished, at first, to make the case as easy as I could: I therefore chose for an example the nominative to a neuter verb, instead of the nominative to an active verb; because in the neuter verb the action does not pass over to any object."

"Then," said Mary, "there is an agent in all sorts of verbs, for there can be no verb without some one to do it; but there need not always be an object."

"No," replied her mother; "if the verb is neuter, the action remains in the agent; and there is no object. Neuter verbs are therefore called intransitive. Thus, to sleep, to cough, to laugh, to cry, are neuter verbs, and have no object."

"To be sure," said Mary, "when I sleep, or cough, or laugh, or cry, I do it all alone, without meddling with any body or any thing. I think, mamma, there ought to be some difference in the ending of the noun, to show whether it is nominative or objective; some sign to point out the case, like the comma in the possessive case."

"In the Latin language the different cases of nouns are formed by their different terminations," said her mother; "but as it is not so in the English language, you must reflect whether the noun performs the action, or is the object of the action."

"Oh yes," said Mary, "the dog barks, the cat purs, the kitten frolics; all these nouns are in the nominative case."

"True," said her mother.

Then Mary continued, "The dog is beaten, the cat is stroked, the kitten is caressed; all these are in the objective case, because"——

"Stop, Mary, you are wrong in your examples of the objective case."

"Why, mamma? Is not the dog the object beaten, the cat the object stroked, and the kitten the object caressed?"

"Certainly, they are the objects beaten, stroked, and caressed; but as they come before the verb, they cannot be in the objective case; for you know that nouns which come before the verb are nominative."

"Well, this is the most difficult thing I have met with in all the grammar," said Mary.

"Since you think so, my dear," said her mother, "we had better finish the lesson for to-day; and we will resume the subject to-morrow, when you will come quite fresh to it."

LESSON XXIII

NOUNS—USES OF CASES

"Pray, mamma," said Mary, "now that I am quite fresh, will you explain to me how I am to make out when the object is in the nominative case, and when it is in the objective case?"

"Nothing can be more easy," replied her mother; "it is simply by observing whether the noun comes before or after the verb. If you say, 'The dog is beaten,' the object, dog, coming before the verb, is in the nominative case. If you say, 'He beats the dog,' the object, dog, coming after the verb, is in the objective case."

"Oh! is that all?" exclaimed Mary, quite delighted that the difficulty was so readily got over; "that is very easy to understand, and therefore it will not be difficult to remember. So, then, it is the verb that settles what case the noun is to be in?"

"Yes," replied her mother; "verbs are said to govern nouns, because they determine their cases. All nouns that come before the verb are in the nominative case; and all those which follow after the verb are in the objective case. The dog is beaten, the cat is stroked. the kitten is caressed, are all objects acted upon; but as they come before the verb, they are in the nominative case."

"That is very clear," said Mary. "Pray, mamma, let me find out some examples how verbs govern nouns. 'Feed the child:' here the governing verb, feed, comes before the noun, child; and obliges it to be in the objective case. 'The child is fed;' here the governing verb, fed, comes after the noun, child, and obliges it to be in the nominative case.'

"Very well," said her mother. "Now give me some examples of active verbs, in which there are two nouns, the one the agent, the other the object, and tell me their cases."

" 'John rides the horse;' 'Sophy eats cherries.' Here John and Sophy, the agents, come before the verb, and are, therefore, nominative; and horse and cherries, the objects, follow the verb, and are, therefore, objective."

"Very well: but if I say, 'The horse is ridden by John;' and 'The cherries are eaten by Sophy;' how would you explain the cases?"

"Oh, now the agents and the objects have changed places; so the horse and cherries become nominative, and John and Sophy objective."

"Observe," said her mother, "that whenever the object comes before the verb, the verb is passive. 'The horse is ridden,' 'The cherries are eaten,' are passive verbs."

"But, mamma, in many passive verbs there is no agent at all; for instance, if you say simply, 'The dog is beaten,' 'The cherries are eaten,' without saying who beat the dog, or who ate the cherries."

"There must, my dear, always be an agent to do the verb; and, if it is not mentioned, it is at least understood."

"It is true," said Mary, laughing; "the dog cannot be beaten, unless some one beats him; nor the cherries eaten, without some one to eat them."

"When that some one is mentioned," continued her mother, "it is always preceded by a preposition; as, 'The dog is beaten *by* John,' 'The cherries are eaten *by* Sophy.'"

"Why, then, the little prepositions seem to govern nouns also?" observed Mary.

"That is true," said her mother; "whenever a noun (or pronoun) is preceded by a preposition, it is obliged to be in the objective case; as, 'John sits *on* the chair;' 'Charles goes *to* papa;' 'I stand *by* the fire;' the prepositions *on, to, by,* cause the nouns *chair, papa,* and *fire,* to be in the objective case."

"And the sense shows them to be in the objective also," said Mary; "for *chair, papa,* and *fire,* are the objects either to sit in, to go to, or to stand by. But I do not think it fair," added she, "that the poor nouns should have two masters. It is very well to be governed by the verbs, for they are parts of speech of great consequence; but it is really too bad for such little insignificant words as prepositions to pretend to govern nouns."

"Yet, so it is, my dear," said her mother, smiling;

"and, I fear, they have no recourse but to submit; we must, therefore, leave them to their fate. I will now write a sentence including all the three cases, to see whether you can distinguish them." She then wrote as follows:—"The baby cries, because she is sleepy, so put her in the cradle; but where is the baby's cradle?"

" 'The *baby*,' " said Mary, "is nominative, because *baby* goes before the governing verb, *'cries.'* "

" '*She is sleepy*;' she is also nominative, because *she* comes before the verb."

" 'Put her in the cradle;' *her* is objective; for *her* comes after the governing verb *put*, and is the object which is put in the cradle. In *'the baby's cradle,' baby's* is in the possessive case, because cradle is something that belongs to the baby."

"What happy nouns those in the possessive case are!" exclaimed Mary; "they have no domineering verbs to govern them."

"Well, my dear," said her mother, "I think you will not easily forget how verbs govern nouns."

"Oh no: I shall fancy that a verb is a great general, who marches in the midst of a troop of nouns, and commands all the soldiers who go before, and all those who follow after him: and that he calls the troops who go before him nominative, and those that follow after him objective."

"And if," said her mother, carrying on the joke, "a noun, instead of joining the army, should send a pronoun in his stead, General Verb would command him also, would he not?"

"To be sure," said Mary, laughing, "verbs govern pronouns as well as nouns."

"I think we may now conclude the subject of nouns. Before taking leave of it, however, I must tell you, that the rule of the nominative coming before the verb, and of the objective following the verb, admits of some few exceptions; which you will learn hereafter."

A STORY

THE SECRET

A Tale

WILLIAM, a little boy of seven years of age, was playing one day in the garden, with his friend George, when the latter, looking round to see that no one was in sight, said to him in a half whisper, "I will tell you a secret, if you will promise to keep it."

"Oh, do!" cried William; "I promise I will not say a single word about it to any body."

George then said that, the following Monday being his birthday, his mamma was preparing a great treat for that day. "First," said he, "we are to drink tea out of doors, under the great trees; but it is not to be tea like other days—only make-believe, milk and water and bread and butter; there is to be real tea, and fruit and cakes, and all sorts of nice things. Then, after that, we are to run about and play at games; and then we are to dance on the grass, for there is to be a fiddler to play to us. Then, when it is dark, we are to go into the house, and a man is to show us the magic lantern. Did you ever see a magic lantern, William? You cannot think how beautiful it is!"

"What is it like?" inquired William.

"Oh, it is pictures, that look as if they were real, and the people alive; it is the most curious thing in the world, for you can only see them in the dark."

"In the dark!" repeated Willy; "how is it possible to see in the dark?"

"Oh, I don't mean you can see in the dark, but only the room must be quite dark; and then there is a light inside the magic lantern to show the pictures. It is very difficult to explain; but you would understand it at once if you saw it. Well, after that we are to go out again in the garden."

"What! all in the dark?"

"Oh, yes! then it must be quite dark every where, for there are to be fireworks."

"I have seen fireworks," said Willy; "they make a light themselves; they are called squibs and crackers."

"Oh! but we are to have very grand fireworks, besides squibs and crackers. We are to have sky-rockets, that fly up into the sky, making such a noise, 'tis enough to frighten you: then, when they get to the top, they turn back and burst all to pieces, and out comes—what do you think?—why, such a number of bright shining stars as you never saw!—a great deal larger than the common stars that are in the sky; and down they fall, twinkle, twinkle, all the while, till they are quite out. Then mamma says, there is to be a Catherine's wheel: I don't know what that is, because I never saw one; but she says it goes round faster than any other wheels, and that it is all made of fire, and of all sorts of colours. Won't that be pretty?"

"Yes," replied William, "to be sure it will; but am I to see it too?"

"Oh dear, yes! you, and Sophy, and Mary, and Emily, and every body is to be invited. Mamma says, we shall be twenty boys and girls; only think what a number!"

"But if so many people are to be there," said William, "what is the use of keeping it a secret?"

"Oh, because mamma says it must be a surprise, and that will make them all like it the better; so mind you keep your promise, and don't tell."

"Oh, yes," said William; "I shall not say one word about it:" and he thought nothing would be so easy as to keep a secret.

When he returned home, his mamma asked him how he had been amused, and what game he had been playing at with George. William, instead of answering immediately, and telling her every thing that had passed, as he was accustomed to do, stood thinking what he should say; for the truth is, both he and George had been so busy talking of the approaching Monday, that they had done nothing else.

After some little time William answered, "I do not recollect playing at any thing; we were only talking."

"It must have been very entertaining conversation," replied she, "to have kept you from play." William coloured: he was afraid he had said something that might lead his mamma to guess the secret, and he felt very uncomfortable that he could not tell her all. This made him look down abashed, and his mother fancied he was ashamed. "I hope, my dear," said she, "that you and George have not been saying any thing wrong?"

"Oh no, mamma,—" and he hesitated, "only—but I must not tell."

"I do not know whether that is quite right; for if you said nothing improper, I know no reason why you should conceal what you talked about."

"Because—because, mamma," said William, "it is a secret;" then fearing he had gone too far, he added, "*saying* it was a secret is not *telling* a secret, is it?"

"No; for I cannot tell what your secret is about; and if you have promised not to tell it, we had better speak no more about it, for fear you should say something that might make me guess what it is." William thought that it was very kind of his mamma not to press him to tell the secret: "if it had been Sophy," said he, "she would never have left off teasing me to tell her all about it."

"Sophy is too young to understand that it is wrong to tell a secret; but I, who know that it is a great fault, and that people who cannot keep a secret are laughed at and despised, would on no account that you should tell me. But perhaps it is better not to be told a secret; they are often troublesome to keep. So let us talk of something else." She then took up a pen and began writing a note; and said, "What I am writing is no secret, so I will tell it you, William, for I am sure it will please you."

"Oh, do, pray, mamma!"

"It is to tell grandmamma, that we shall go and spend the day with her on Monday;" and she looked up to see how pleased William would be, but William's countenance expressed nothing but concern and disappointment.

"Why are you not glad, William?"

"I like going to see grandmamma," said William; "but why must you go on Monday?"

"And why not on Monday?" replied his mother: "it is a day on which I have no engagement."

"But," said William, hesitating and colouring, "perhaps you *may* have an invitation, mamma."

"Then I should refuse it, my dear; for when I have sent this note to your grandmamma, I shalt be engaged to her."

Poor William sighed: he knew not what to say; the invitation to George's party would come too late, and he would not be able to go! He stood intently watching his mother while she finished the note, folded it up, and directed it.

"Light me the little candle, William," said she, "to seal it." But William was so wrapped up in his thoughts, that he scarcely heard her.

"Why, my dear," exclaimed she, "what is the matter? This is very whimsical." She then lighted the taper herself; and having sealed the note, rang for a servant to carry it. When William found that the note was on the point of going, he could refrain no longer, and bursting into tears, he sobbed out, "Must I then tell you, mamma?"

"Tell me what, my dear child?" said she, tenderly caressing him; "yes, tell me any thing that grieves you."

"What! my secret?" exclaimed he.

"Oh, no, stop," she cried; "not a word of your secret; you have promised, and must not tell it, even to me, however it may grieve you."

"Oh dear! I will never promise to keep a secret any more."

"Then you must never hear one," returned his mother; "for if you do, you are bound to keep it."

"Well, I will keep it, mamma; but then pray don't send your letter."

"What can my letter have to do with your secret? However, I will not ask questions you ought not to answer."

The servant came into the room, but his mother did not give him the letter; she only desired him to put some coals on the fire. William felt quite relieved: he sprung up on his mother's lap; and, putting his arms round her neck, kissed her tenderly.

Soon after the servant came in again with a note from George's mother, Mrs. Middleton, saying that the servant who brought it waited for an answer. "Oh! read it, mamma," cried William, quite overjoyed: "read it quick; it is the secret." His mother read the note, and the secret was at once explained. "Well, William," said she, smiling, "I suppose I may write to accept this invitation, and you will not object to John's taking this letter."

"Oh, no," cried William; "I am so glad the other letter is not gone; and so glad the secret is over. I thought it was great fun to have a secret, but now I think it very disagreeable. I hate secrets, but I like parties, mamma, without secrets; and I am very glad we shall go to George's birthday treat."

LESSON XXIV

PERSONAL PRONOUNS

"In our former lesson on pronouns, Mary, I taught you their meaning generally."

"Yes, mamma, they are the words that are put in the place of nouns, and point out the noun without naming it."

"We shall now divide them into classes. The first and most important of these are the personal pronouns."

"Those," said Mary, "must be the pronouns used instead of the names of persons; as, *I, you, he, she,* and *who* are obliged to obey General Verb, just the same as nouns are. Then I remember the pronoun *it,* which is used in the place of things."

"I conclude that you also recollect the meaning of the singular and plural numbers."

"Oh yes, we talked much about them. The singular means one single person or thing; and the plural, several—perhaps only a few—perhaps a great many, but always more than one."

"Well, my dear, there are three persons in the singular number, and three in the plural."

"What do you mean?" exclaimed Mary. "There cannot be three persons in the singular number, if the singular number means one single person. And there must be a great many more than three persons in the plural, for the plural may mean all the persons in the whole world."

"True," said her mother, smiling, "a great many more; but all these persons are divided by grammarians into three classes, so that the three classes form the three persons. The first class consists of those who speak; the second of those who are spoken to; and the third of those who are spoken of."

"But, mamma, every body can speak, except some few, perhaps, who may be dumb."

"True; but some listen while others speak, else they would speak to no purpose."

"Oh! to be sure, somebody must hear what they say, or it would be useless for them to talk."

"Well, those who speak are said to be of the first person. If it is one person who speaks, and speaks of himself alone, he uses the pronoun *I*, and says, *I* am tired, *I* have been walking. If he speaks of more than one person, the pronoun *we* is used; as, *we* are hungry, *we* are going to dinner."

"Then, I suppose," said Mary, "the people who are spoken to, and belong to the second class, are of the second person?"

"Yes: and what pronoun would you use in speaking to people?"

"I say *you*, if I speak to a single person; as, will *you* walk? are *you* hungry? and if I speak to several persons, I use the pronoun—I declare I do not know what pronoun I ought to use, mamma! I believe it is *you* also; but can *you* be singular and plural both?"

"Yes," replied her mother. "Properly speaking, *you* is a plural pronoun; but it has become customary to use it in the singular number also. Many years ago the pronoun 'thou' was used when applied to a single person; as, *thou* readest well. But this pronoun is no longer used in common discourse, except by Quakers."

"Oh, yes, you know Mr. Barker always says *thou* and *thee:* it sounds so odd. When he came here the other day, he said to me, 'Is thy mother at home? Wilt thou tell her I am come to see her?' Then, in the Bible, mamma, thou and thee are used."

"Yes; we, who are not Quakers, use those pronouns only for sacred writings, thinking that it gives a greater solemnity to the style; and in conversation we use the pronoun *you*, both in the singular and in the plural."

"And what is the third person, mamma?" asked Mary.

"The third person," said her mother, "is the person or thing spoken of. In the singular number, *he, she,* and *it* are used, and *they* in the plural."

"But how can *it* be a personal pronoun, mamma; for it does not stand for a person, but for a thing?"

"Things," replied her mother, "belong to the third class, and are, therefore, considered as being of the third person. They cannot be of the first person, because they cannot speak."

"No, indeed," said Mary, laughing; "they have neither mouth nor tongue to speak with, and they cannot be of the second person, because they have no ears to hear; so it would be nonsense speaking to them: but it is true they may be of the third person, because we speak about them. We talk of frocks, and shoes, and dolls, and tables, and chairs, and——"

"Well, Mary," said her mother, interrupting her, "I think you have given plenty of examples. Now try if you can give examples of the three persons, *he, she,* and *it.*"

"That is, of the three third persons," said Mary. "*He is gone out riding; she came to see me; it is very pretty.*"

"Very well; you see that pronouns have genders as well as nouns."

"Oh yes; they must have the same genders as the nouns they stand for; *he* is masculine: *she* is feminine; and *it* is of the neuter gender."

"The third person of the plural number, *they,* suits all the genders equally well; for you may say, *they* are wise men; *they* are pretty girls; and *they* are sweet oranges." Mary's mother then took a pen, and wrote down the personal pronouns, as follows:—

	Singular	Plural
First person	I	We
Second person	Thou	You
Third person	He, or She, or It	They

190

But, mamma, these people must all be doing something; for pronouns without any thing else have no sense."

"The pronouns," replied her mother, "are all doing verbs, and the different persons show who it is that is doing the verb. You may say,—

I write,	We sing,
Thou readest,	You drink,
He walks,	They eat;

or," continued she, "if the verb is passive, they are receiving it instead of doing it; as,

I am loved,	We are beaten,
Thou art hated,	You are scolded,
He is praised,	They are praised."

"But, mamma, you said that *thou* was no longer commonly used, except in religious books."

"That is true; but it still keeps its place in grammars."

"Mamma," said Mary, "I have just thought of something that puzzles me sadly. When you say *it* rains, what noun does *it* stand for? Does it mean that the clouds rain?"

"No; for in that case you would say, *they* rain, not *it* rains; you can never use a pronoun in the singular number, for a noun in the plural. The word *it* is used in this as in many other verbs, without standing for any noun, and seems to refer to some cause, or state of things, which makes the rain or hail fall, or thunder roll, or lightning flash. But this is too difficult for you, Mary: I shall therefore only tell you, that the verbs, *it rains, it hails, it thunders, it lightens,* and all others, which have no other nominative than the pronoun *it,* are called impersonal, because there are no persons belonging to them."

"To be sure," said Mary, "you cannot say, I rain, or you hail, or she thunders, or they lighten. Oh! but, mamma, you may say Jupiter thunders."

"True, but then the verb is no longer impersonal.— Well, Mary, *it* is very fine now; so go and take a run in the garden; for *it* is very pleasant to run about after a lesson."

"But pray, mamma," said Mary, "first tell me, have pronouns cases like nouns?"

"The personal pronouns have," replied her mother; "standing in the place of nouns, they undergo the changes which nouns do, whether it be of number, gender, or case. The pronouns which I have just written down are of the nominative case, for they are supposed either to be or to do something."

"Yes," said Mary, "I write is doing something, and I am loved is being something."

LESSON XV

POSSESSIVE PRONOUNS

"Pray, mamma," said Mary, at the next lesson, "have pronouns cases, like nouns?"

"Yes," replied her mother, "as they are put in the place of nouns, they must undergo all the changes which nouns do, whether it be of number, gender, or case. The pronouns I wrote down yesterday are of the nominative case; for they are supposed either to do, or be something; and if you bring them into a sentence, you will find that they come before the verb; as, I eat, thou sleepest, he is happy; we are tired, you speak, they walk. Now, Mary, do you think you could find out a pronoun in the possessive case?"

"Is it like the possessive case of nouns, mamma, written with an *s*, and a comma before it?"

"It is the same case, and has the same meaning, but it is not written in the same manner. How would you express yourself, to say that you possessed any thing; this thimble, for instance?" said she, holding up Mary's thimble.

"I should say," answered Mary, "this thimble belongs to me."

"That denotes possession, it is true, but it is in rather a roundabout way: you use the phrase *belongs to me*, instead of expressing the same meaning by a single pronoun. Is it not shorter and more easy to say, this thimble is *mine?*"

"Oh yes, certainly," said Mary, "*mine* means, belongs to me; how stupid it was of me not to think of *mine!* it is a word I repeat so often. So, then, *mine* is the possessive pronoun for the first person singular."

"Yes; but there is also another possessive pronoun for the first person singular, which is still shorter than mine. If I say this is *my* book, it means that I possess the book, just the same as if I said this book is *mine*."

Then," said Mary, "there are two possessive pronouns for the first person singular."

"Yes; and so there are for the second person singular, *thy* and *thine*, and also for the third, which are, *his*, *hers*, and *its*. All these pronouns, you know, mean possession."

"Yes," said Mary, "you may say, *his* hat, *her* cap. Then, if it is a thing you are speaking of—a tree, for instance—you may say, *its* branches, or *its* blossoms; and of a table, *its* legs. But should not a comma be put before the *s* in *its*, mamma, as it is with nouns in the possessive case?"

"No; the comma is not required, because *it* is never

plural; the possessive case cannot, therefore, be mistaken for the plural number, as it might be with nouns."

"And, pray, what are the plural pronouns in this case?"

"*Our, ours,* for the first person; *your,* or *yours,* for the second person; and *their,* or *theirs,* for the third person."

"But why are there two possessive pronouns for each person?" inquired Mary; "I should have thought that one would have been enough; for if I say this is *my* hat, or this hat is *mine,* it seems to mean the same thing."

"Very nearly, but not quite," replied her mother; "*mine* is used when the noun comes before the pronoun; as, this hat is *mine;* and *my* is used when the noun follows the pronoun; as, this is *my* hat. And it is also the same with the third person feminine," said her mother; "you may say, this glove is *hers,* or this is *her* glove. But there is only one pronoun, *his,* for the third person masculine."

"Well, I wonder there should not be two possessive pronouns for men as well as for women," exclaimed Mary.

"It would certainly be more regular; for you are obliged to use the word *his,* both before and after the noun; as, that is *his* horse, that horse is *his.*"

"I have heard Sophy's nurse say *his'n* sometimes, mamma."

"And she also says *her'n,* instead of hers; and *our'n, your'n, their'n,* instead of ours, yours, and theirs; but this manner of speaking, though it may have been usual a great many years ago, is no longer so except with illiterate people, and you must be careful not to imitate it. Now, try to give me some examples of the way in which the possessive pronouns plural are used."

"Let me see," said Mary, thoughtfully; "you said they were, *our, ours, your, yours, their, theirs.*" Then she went on thus:—

"Will you walk in *our* garden? This garden is *ours.* You see, mamma, I have taken care to say *our* before the garden, and *ours* after it."

"Very well; now for the second person plural."

"If this is not *your* bonnet," said Mary, "which is *yours?* Shall I go on with the third person?"

"Yes, if you please."

"*Their* master teaches them very cleverly;—but, mamma," said Mary, interrupting herself, "children do not possess their master, he does not belong to them, like the garden or the bonnet?"

"Very true," replied her mother; "when you talk of a master who teaches you, a tradesman who serves you with goods, or a doctor who attends you when you are ill, you only mean to say, that you employ or make use of them, not that you possess them."

"Indeed," replied Mary, "I think we belong to the master, more than he belongs to us, for you know we must mind all he says, and do all he bids us."

"And," said her mother, "in speaking of you, he calls

196

you *his* pupils; meaning, that you belong to him, for the purpose of being taught by him. But I am sorry to say," continued she, "that there are some countries where men and women are bought and sold, and belong to their master, just as horses do, and are often as severely whipped as they are. This is when the poor negroes of Africa are made slaves, and sold to work in the sugar and cotton plantations in the West Indies and America."

"How shocking!" exclaimed Mary: "and little children too?"

"Yes, even the little children; but, thank God! slavery exists now in very few countries, and is not permitted in any belonging to England."

"But, mamma, when you say *my* children, it means that we belong to you, though we are not slaves."

"Yes, my love, you and your brothers and sisters belong to us, much more nearly than pupils belong to their master, and you obey us from affection, as well as duty; but when I talk of my mantua-maker, my baker, or my washerwoman, I mean merely to say that I employ them, not that they belong to me."

"Now that you have finished the pronouns of the possessive case, I will tell you what those of the objective case are. Of the singular number, they are, *me, thee, him, her, it.* These pronouns all denote the object of a verb; as, give the book to *me.*"

"Yes," said Mary, "*book* is the object given."

"Remember, my dear, that you are to point out the objective pronoun, and not the noun; so think again."

Mary thought again, and then said, "Oh yes, I was quite wrong. *Me* is the object to whom the book is given. Speak to *him; him* is the object spoken to, and is in the objective case. Go with *her;* stay with *us;* walk with *them.* Then, mamma, all these pronouns follow the verb, as the nouns do in the objective case; so I shall easily be able to distinguish them from the nominative pronouns."

Her mother then wrote out a table of the personal pronouns, with their several cases:

Singular Number

	Nominative	Possessive	Objective
1st Person	I	My, Mine	Me
2nd Person	Thou	Thy, Thine	Thee
3rd Person M & F	He, She	His, Her, Hers	Him, Her
3rd Person Neuter	It	Its	It

Plural Number

	Nominative	Possessive	Objective
1st Person	We	Our, Ours	Us
2nd Person	You	Your, Yours	You
3rd Person	They	Their, Theirs	Them

"You may get this table by heart, Mary, now that you can understand it."

"Indeed, mamma," replied she, "I should have found it a very hard task to have learnt it by heart before you had explained it; for the words are so much alike in their meaning, that I am sure I should have been sadly puzzled to recollect the order in which they were to be repeated."

"We have now finished the personal pronouns," said her mother; "but there are several other classes to be examined, which we will reserve for another day. To-morrow, I shall give you another story."

"I should like so much another story about the beautiful Fairy, Instruction," said Mary.

"That will not be difficult to obtain," replied her mother; "for Instruction is always ready to tell you a story when you will attend to her. We will wait till to-morrow, and then see what she will say to us."

A STORY

THE COAT AND BUTTONS

A Fairy Tale

EDWARD thought, like you, Mary, that he should be very glad to see the fairy again; and one day that he was longing for her she suddenly appeared before him. She showed him some of the curious pages of her glass book, and then asked him what she should animate to give an account of itself.

Edward was much at a loss to determine; he thought first of one thing, then of another, and after being undecided for some time, he said, "I think it would be very funny to hear my coat speak."

Instruction touched his coat with her wand, and then disappeared; and a few moments afterwards a soft voice issued from the bosom of his coat and spoke as follows:—

"I recollect once growing on the back of a sheep."— Though Edward expected to hear the coat speak, he could not help starting back with surprise; however, he interrupted him, saying, "I am afraid, Mr. Coat, you do not know what you are talking about; for coats do

200

not grow, nor do sheep wear coats." "I was only wool when I grew on the sheep," replied the voice; "and a very pleasant life we led together, spending all the day in the green fields, and resting at night on the grass. Sometimes, indeed, the sheep rubbed himself so roughly against the trees and gates, that I was afraid of being torn off; and sometimes the birds came and pecked off a few flakes of the wool to line their nests, and make them soft and warm for their young; but they took so little that I could easily spare it. We had long led this quiet life together, when one day there was a great alarm. The shepherd and his dog drove all the sheep into a fold, and then took them out one by one, and washed them in a stream of water which ran close by. The sheep on which I grew was sadly frightened when his turn came; and, for my part, I could not imagine what they were going to do with me, they rubbed and scrubbed me so much; but when it was over, I looked so delicately white, that I was quite vain of my beauty, and I thought we were now to return and frisk and gambol in the meadow, as we had done before. But, alas, the sheep and I were going to be parted for ever! and I was never more to behold the fresh grass on which I had rested with so much pleasure. Instead of setting the sheep at liberty, the shepherd took out a large pair of shears.—Only imagine our terror!—the poor sheep, I believe, thought his head was going to be cut off, and began to bleat most piteously; but the shepherd, without attending to his cries, held him down, and began cutting me off close to his skin. When the sheep found that the shears did not hurt him, he remained quiet; it was then my turn to be frightened. It is true that the shears did not hurt me either, because I could not feel; but then I could not bear the thoughts of being parted from my dear friend, the sheep: for we had grown up together ever since he had been a little lamb. The sheep, who could feel, suffered even more than I did from the separation. As soon as he was released, he went about shivering with cold, bleating and moaning for the kiss of his beloved fleece. As for me, I was packed in a bag with a great many other fleeces, and sent to some mills, where there were a number of strange little things that were for ever twisting and turning round. They seized hold of us, and pulled us, and twisted us about in such a wonderful manner, that at last we were all drawn out into worsted threads, so unlike wool, that I hardly knew myself again. But it was still worse, when, some time afterwards, they plunged me into a large copper of dark dirty-looking water; and when I was taken out, instead of being white, I was of a bright blue colour, and looked very beautiful. Well, some time after this I was sent to the cloth mills, and my threads were stretched in a machine called a loom, and there I was woven into a piece of cloth. I was then folded up, and lay quiet for some time."

"Indeed," said Edward, "I think you wanted a little rest, after going through so many changes."

"Soon after," resumed the voice, "I was bought by a tailor, and lay on the shelf of his shop, when one day you and your papa came in and asked to see some cloth to make you a coat. I was taken down and unfolded on the counter with several other pieces, and, if you remember, you chose me on account of my beautiful colour."

"So I did," said Edward; "but you are not so bright a blue now as you were then."

"Something the worse for wear," replied the coat; "if you stain me and cover me with dust, that is your fault, not mine. But to conclude my story; the tailor took out his enormous scissors, which reminded me of the shears that had separated me from the sheep, and cut me into the shape of a coat. I was then sewed up by some journeymen, who sat cross-legged on a table; and, when I was finished, I was sent to you; and, ever since, I have covered the back of a little inquisitive boy, instead of that of a sheep."

Edward was much entertained with the story of the coat. "But these bright buttons," said he, "are not made of wool; have you nothing to say about them?"

"They were perfect strangers to me till they were sewn on," said the coat; "I know nothing about them: they must speak for themselves."

Upon this, the whole row of buttons raised their sharp voices at once, which sounded like the jingling of so many little bells. This made such a confused noise, that Edward could not distinguish a word they said. He, therefore, in an imperative tone, commanded silence; and, laying hold of one of them with his finger and thumb, he said, "Come, Mr. Button, let me hear the story from you, while all the rest remain quiet." Pleased by this preference, the face of the button that was spoken to shone brighter than usual, and in a small, shrill, but distinct voice, he began thus:—

"We lay for a long time under ground, not bright

and shining as you now see us, but mixed up with dirt and rubbish. How long we remained there it is impossible for me to say; for, as it was always dark, there was no telling day from night, nor any means of counting weeks and years."

"But could not you hear the church clock strike?" said Edward; "that would have told you how time passed."

"Oh no," replied the button; "if we had had ears, we could not have heard, so deep were we buried in the bowels of the earth."

"Oh dear! how, dismal that must have been!" exclaimed Edward.

"Not for us, who neither thought nor felt," replied the button. "Well, after having lain there for ages, perhaps, all at once there was an opening made in the ground, and men came down where we lay, and dug us up. They talked about a fine vein of copper. 'I am glad we have reached it at last,' said they. 'It will repay us all our labour.' They then put us into the basket, and we were taken up above ground, and into daylight. The glare of light was so strong to us, who had been so long in utter darkness, that, if we had had eyes, it would almost have blinded us. Well, after that, we were put into a fiery furnace."

"I am sure you must have been glad then that you could not feel," said Edward; "and were you burnt to ashes?"

"Oh no," replied the button; "copper is a metal,

and metals will not burn; but we were melted: and as the earth and rubbish which were mixed with us do not melt, we ran out through some holes that were made on purpose for us to escape from our dirty companions, who were not fit society for us. We were then imprisoned in moulds, where we were left to cool and become solid again. Men then came with hammers, and beat us till we became quite flat. Every time they struck us, we hallooed out as loud as we could, and our cries resounded to a great distance; but they went on all the same."

"What!" exclaimed Edward; "had you voices to cry out?"

"No," replied the button; "but do you not know that if you strike against metal it rings or resounds? The sound of a bell is nothing but the metal tongue striking against the inside of the bell; and you know what a noise it makes." Just then the dinner bell began ringing, and Edward cried out, "That it does, indeed."

"Well," continued the button, "after we had been beaten into flat sheets, we were sent to the turner's, who cut us into little bits, and then placed us, one after the other, into a strange kind of machine, called a lathe: he held us there while he turned a wheel with his foot so fast that it would have made one giddy."

"That is, if you had had a head to be giddy," said Edward laughing.

"When I was taken out of the lathe, I was quite surprised to see what a pretty round shape I had; I wondered what was to be done to me next; for as there was nothing by which I could be sewn on to a coat, I did not think that I was to be made into a button, but supposed I was intended for a piece of money."

"Yes; a round flat button is something like a sixpence," said Edward; "but then you were not made of silver."

"True; and I soon found that I was to be a button; for they fastened a tail to me, and rubbed me for a great length of time till I became very bright. I was then stuck with the rest of us on a sheet of thick white paper."

"Oh! I remember," cried Edward; "you were all stuck on the paper, when the tailor showed you to papa and me, and you looked quite beautiful." Edward then listened in expectation of the button continuing his story, but it was ended, and his voice was gone.

From this time it was observed that Edward took more care of his coat than usual; and, when from any accident he dirtied it, he brushed it quite clean, and now and then he was seen rubbing the buttons to make them shine bright.

LESSON XXVI

RELATIVE PRONOUNS

At the next lesson of grammar, Mary came skipping into the room with her book in her hand, saying, "Now, mamma, for the rest of the pronouns."

"The next class of pronouns," said her mother, "is called *relative*, because they relate to some word said before. There are but three relative pronouns, *who*, *which*, and *that*."

"They will be very easy to remember, mamma, being so few."

"But, Mary, I do not mean that you should remember them like a parrot; you must understand them, and then you would remember them equally well, were there few or many. In order to understand them, you must know to what words they relate. If I say, the man *who* brought me a letter, to what word does *who* relate?"

"To the man, certainly."

"Very well; I will now give you a more complicated example. The tree *that* was blown down yesterday fell near Charles, *who* was sadly frightened."

"*That* relates to the tree," said Mary, "but *who* relates

207

to Charles being frightened. Now mamma," added she, "it is my turn to give an example."

"Well, my dear, think of one; and try to introduce in it all the three pronouns."

Mary thought for a long time, looking very grave all the while, and at last she said—"Do you remember the pretty doll *that* grandmamma gave me, *which* has long ringlets? I have lent it to Sophy, *who* is very fond of playing with it."

"Very well; but what made you look so grave, my dear? I expected you would say something very serious, instead of talking about playing with dolls."

"Oh, mamma! it is so difficult to find out how to place the pronouns, that one cannot help looking grave, even when one is thinking of something amusing."

"Well, now, Mary," said her mother, "you may be really grave; for I am going to teach you a very hard word."

Mary looked very serious, and listened with great attention to her mother, who proceeded—

"The word to which the pronoun relates is called the *antecedent*, which means something that goes before; can you remember that word?"

"Oh yes; it is not so difficult as I thought, when you told me to be so grave. I shall remember the word *antecedent*, because it is like the ante-chamber, before you go into the drawing-room."

"Now, then," said her mother, "I will give you a

sentence, in which you shall find out the nouns that are antecedents to their relative pronouns. 'The sheep which were feeding on the common were scared by a little boy, who ran hallooing after them, and the dog that guarded them had much ado to bring them back.' "

"*Sheep*," said Mary, after a thoughtful pause, "is the antecedent of *which; boy* is the antecedent of *who;* and *dog* the antecedent of *that.* How foolish it was," continued she, "for such large animals as sheep to be afraid of a little boy! And pray, mamma, have the relative pronouns numbers, and genders, and cases, like the personal pronouns?"

"*Which* and *that,*" replied her mother, "never change: but *who* has the three cases. The possessive case of *who* is *whose,* and the objective *whom.* Thus you might ask, *who* called here yesterday? and I should answer, a lady *whom* I saw, but *whose* name I forget: can you tell me the cases of these three pronouns?"

"Yes, I believe I can," said Mary; "in the first place, they all relate to the lady. *Who* is nominative; *whom* must be the objective, because the lady was the object spoken to; and *whose* is the possessive case, because the lady must have a name, though you forget it, mamma," said Mary, laughing.

"True," replied her mother. "The pronouns *who, whose,* and *whom* are used in general for rational beings; that is, men, women, and children. *Which* and *that* are more correctly applied to animals and things. You do not say the horse *who* trotted, or the tree *who* is in blossom; but the horse *that* trotted, and the tree *which* is in blossom."

"And would it be wrong to say, the tree *that* is in blossom?"

"No: the pronoun *that* may be applied to all sorts of nouns; for you may say the child *that* played with the flower *that* I gathered, and the box *that* I opened, with equal propriety. But, as the pronoun *who* is in general confined to rational beings, it is considered more appropriate to them than the pronoun *that*. Relative pronouns, when they are used to ask questions, are called interrogative pronouns; as, *Who* is that? To *whom* did you speak? *Whose* carriage is that?"

"I shall always know them," said Mary, "by the note of interrogation, *Which* book shall I read in? *What* work shall I do? But then, mamma, these pronouns are both relative and interrogative."

"Yes," replied her mother; "but they cannot be both at the same time, for they have different meanings as a relative, or as an interrogative pronoun. When it relates to an antecedent, as 'The book *which* I read,' it is a relative pronoun; but when it asks a question, as, 'Which book will you read in?' it is interrogative. We shall now finish the lesson," continued her mother; "but we must have one more on pronouns, before we come to our story."

The thought of a story always gave Mary courage to get through the difficult parts of her lesson. It is true that parsing the story obliged her sometimes to work hard; but she knew that nothing could be learned well without taking pains. Then she was really fond of learning new things, and she thought any trouble better than being ignorant.

LESSON XXVII

DEMONSTRATIVE PRONOUNS

"THE next class of pronouns is the *demonstrative*. They are *this*, *these*, *that*, and *those*. They are called demonstrative because they *demonstrate*, that is, point out the noun before which they are placed; as, *this* orange is very sweet."

"Yes," said Mary; "this marks out the noun orange, which is very sweet."

"I will give you another example," said her mother; "*that* apple is sour. Now, let me see if you can find out one."

"*These* plums are ripe," said Mary, "*those* nuts are hard. When we use the demonstrative pronoun, it seems as if we were pointing our finger to show the things we are speaking of; but I am afraid that I shall be puzzled to distinguish the demonstrative from the relative pronoun, because they both point to nouns."

"Observe," said her mother, "that they point different ways, so that the very circumstance of pointing which you thought would perplex you, will help you to distinguish them. The relative pronoun points

212

backwards to the noun; as, 'The horse *which* I rode,' whilst the demonstrative, as, '*Those* men,' points forwards to the noun."

"Oh yes," said Mary, quite pleased to have it so easily explained, "*which* points backwards to the noun horse; and *those* points forwards to the noun man; so *which* is a relative pronoun, and *those* a demonstrative pronoun. To be sure, the relative must point backwards to its antecedent, and the demonstrative forwards to its _____ its what mamma? Is there no corresponding word for the noun the demonstrative pronoun points out?"

"I believe not," replied her mother.

"Then I think there ought to be," said Mary.

"Let me see now," said her mother, "whether you can introduce the demonstrative pronouns, *this*, *that*, *these*, and *those*, into a sentence."

Mary thought a little and then said, "I am going to put the room in order, mamma; I will place *these* chairs round *this* table, and put *those* prints on *that* table."

"Very well: do you understand the difference between *this* table and *that* table?"

"There is a great deal of difference," said Mary, looking at them: "one is square, and the other is round; then this table is large, and that is small."

"And do the pronouns *this* and *that* point out the difference between the tables?"

"Oh no," said Mary, laughing; "the adjectives do that: *this* does not mean a large round table, and *that* a small square one; for if you said *this* table and *that* table, without my seeing them, I should not know at all of what shape or size they were."

"Then, what do *this* table and *that* table mean?"

"*This*," replied Mary, "means the table nearest to us, and *that* the table farther off."

"Ah! now you are right," said her mother, "and I dare say you will be able to tell me what *these* and *those* mean?"

"The same thing, mamma, only they are plural instead of singular. *These* chairs are nearer to us than *those* prints. I like *these* apples better than *those* I ate yesterday." Mary then ran to the piano, and began playing a waltz; her mother waited patiently till she had finished it; but then she began another, and her mother inquired how many waltzes she meant to play before she went on with her lesson.

"Only two," replied Mary. "I wanted to tell you that I did not like *this* waltz so well as *that* I played first."

Her mother smiled at her example, and said, "So, then, you are practising your lesson of grammar on the piano! Well, then, I shall leave you to finish it there," and she went away.

LESSON XXVIII

TIME AND PLACE

"I GOT into a sad puzzle with the example of my waltzes, mamma," said Mary, "when you left me. I could not make out how one waltz could be farther off than the other, when they were both played on the same piano?"

"They are both at the same distance in regard to place, my dear, certainly; but not in regard to time, for you played the one before you played the other."

"Then, there are two farther-offs?" said Mary.

"Yes: the one relates to time, and the other to place; you may say next year is a distant time, and York is a distant place."

"Oh yes," said Mary; "the one means, that there is a great deal of ground between you and York; and the other ——"

"Stop, Mary," said her mother, interrupting her; "let us understand well what one distance means before we explain the other. If I say America is a very distant country, there is something else besides ground between us and America."

"Yes, a great deal of water; all the Atlantic Ocean; well, I mean the quantity of land and water there is between us and that country."

"And if I should say the moon is very distant, how would you explain it? for there is neither land nor water between us and the moon."

"No, but it is a very long way off; and there is nothing between us and the moon that I know of, or at least nothing but air."

"Well, my dear, all these distances, whether they consist of land, water, air, or any thing else, can be expressed by one single word, *space*. I may say there is a great space between us and America; and a still greater between us and the moon."

"It is very convenient," said Mary, "to have one word to say so many things; and are small distances called spaces too?"

"Yes: you may say the space between those two chairs; or, those books will not take up much space on the shelf."

Oh, dear mamma!" cried Mary, with the pleased look of having made a discovery, "I have just thought of some little tiny spaces, much smaller still. In music books, you know, there are five lines and four spaces between them;" and she pointed them out to her mother in a book which lay open on the piano.

"Yes, Mary: and they are so called because they are the spaces or distances between the lines. In regard to time, distance also means far off; but it means far off in point of time. I may say next Thursday is a distant day, or next year is very distant, and the next century is more distant still."

"I understand the difference very well now, mamma."

"Then can you tell me how you measure the distance of space?"

"Why," said Mary, pausing to reflect, "I have seen you measure the distance from one end of the room to the other with a foot measure; and a yard measure is longer, and will measure more quickly. Then I remember, when you measured the length of the gravel-walk, you did it with a long string."

"True, but I measured the string first, otherwise I could not have known how long the walk was."

"But, mamma, if you were to measure the space between this place and London, it would be very tedious to do it with a foot rule, a yard, or even a long string, for you know it is seventy miles—*miles*," repeated she, a new thought suddenly occurring, "miles are the very thing,—that is, I mean milestones; for the distance from here to London is marked by milestones."

"True; but recollect," said her mother, "the ground must be measured first, in order to know where the milestones are to be placed. Now can you find out how to measure the distance of time?"

"No, indeed," said Mary; "feet, and yards, and miles, will not measure time."

"Cannot you tell me how long it will be from this time to your dinner-time?"

"Oh yes; it is now ten o'clock, and I dine at two; so there are four hours from this to my dinner-time."

"You see, then, that you can measure time by a clock, even with less trouble than you can measure space by a foot or yard. Time is divided into seconds, minutes, hours, days, and years, and a clock or a watch is an instrument for the purpose of measuring time."

"They may do very well for hours, and even for days, perhaps; but for years, mamma! surely there ought to be a greater measure to measure years with, something like the milestones, that measure very long spaces."

"And so there is, Mary: when you are old enough to understand it, you will find that there is something like milestones in the sky to measure time with."

Mary stared with astonishment; she longed extremely to know what sort of things these milestones could be; she looked up to the sky, but could discover nothing that bore any resemblance to milestones. She then intreated her mother to tell her what it was.

Her mother smiled, and, pointing to the sun, said, "That is one of the milestones."

"Oh, mamma! you are joking now," exclaimed Mary.

"No, indeed, my dear. The sun served to measure time long before clocks and watches were invented; and even now, the labourers in the field, who have not watches, learn, by observing whereabouts the sun is in the sky, when it is time for them to begin their day's work, or when it is twelve o'clock, for them to go to dinner. When you are older, Mary, you will learn that the sun and stars are indeed the only true measures of time, and that our clocks and watches, when they go wrong, are set according to them; but this is too difficult for you now; besides, it does not belong to a lesson of grammar,—indeed we have been talking of other subjects almost the whole of the lesson."

"Oh! but, mamma, I think I have learned a great deal about time and space, and I am sure it has amused me."

"Well, that must serve as an apology for deviating so much from our subject. It is too late to return to the grammar to-day, so we will reserve the remainder of the pronouns for the next lesson."

LESSON XXIX

OTHER TYPES OF PRONOUNS

"WELL, Mary," said her mother, "we must keep close to our subject to-day, in order to finish the demonstrative pronouns."

"I remember, mamma, that I was just going to ask you a question about them, when time and space interrupted us. Is the word *that* both a relative and a demonstrative pronoun? for you have named *that* in both these classes of pronouns."

"Yes, my dear, it is; but the meaning of the word in one class is so different from its meaning in the other that you will not easily confound them."

"It must be quite different, indeed; for the *relative* pronoun *that* relates to some noun gone before, and called its antecedent; and the *demonstrative* pronoun *that* points out some noun that follows after. Do not I recollect well, mamma?" said she, with a look of self-approbation.

"Very well," said her mother.

"Now," continued Mary, "I will tell you what it was that helped me out. It was the pointing backwards and forwards; for when I am thinking of the relative and

220

demonstrative pronouns, I fancy I see a man pointing with his finger either backwards or forwards. When the pronoun is relative, he points with one hand backwards to the noun, as the hoop *which* I trundled; and when the pronoun is demonstrative, he points with the other hand forwards to the noun, as *that* house is handsome."

Her mother smiled and said, "I advise you to draw his picture to imprint it on your memory; but as a pronoun can never be both relative and demonstrative at the same time, it cannot point both ways at once, therefore it is not necessary that the man should use both his hands."

"Oh I am glad of that," said Mary, "for hands are very difficult to draw; so I shall put my pronoun in profile, and show but one hand and arm."

"Now," said her mother, "I will place the two *thats* in one sentence; and we shall see whether you will be able to distinguish the relative from the demonstrative: is *that* work *that* you are doing very amusing?"

"The first *that*," said Mary, "is demonstrative, because it points forwards to the noun work; and the second *that* is relative, because it points backwards to the noun work. Now, mamma, let me put the two *thats* in a sentence;" and, observing a horse pass the window, she said, "*that* horse is the same *that* galloped by yesterday."

"Very well; but can you tell me what is the antecedent to the relative *that?*"

"I do not know," said Mary, "for horse belongs to the demonstrative pronoun; so I suppose it is not horse?"

"Not the word horse which is named in the sentence, but that which is understood: when you say *the same*, it is clear the same *horse* is meant."

"Oh yes," said Mary; "the word being unnecessary is left out, as you told me in the last lesson."

"Now, Mary, what will you say when I tell you that the word *that*, besides being both a relative and a demonstrative pronoun, is also sometimes a conjunction?"

"Oh, mamma!" exclaimed Mary, "that is too bad. It must be very puzzling for one word to have three different meanings."

"It requires, at least, more sense to understand them, and more attention to be able to distinguish between them, than, perhaps, can be expected from a little girl of your age."

"Well, but let met try," cried Mary, who was ambitious of not being considered as a very little girl. "Pray give me an example, mamma."

"Here is one," replied her mother: "I am so tired *that* I can hardly stand. What is the meaning of *that* in this sentence?"

"It does not point to any noun, either backwards or forwards, so it can neither be a relative nor a demonstrative pronoun. I suppose, therefore, it is a conjunction."

"Yes; *that* joins two parts of a sentence together, as, 'I am so tired *that* I can hardly stand;' and shows their connection, which is, *that* I can hardly stand, because I am so tired."

"Now let me find out an example, mamma. 'She is so sorry for her fault, *that* I do not think she will ever do it again.' Suppose, mamma, that we were to put the three *thats* all in one sentence; but that is too difficult for me, you must do it."

Mamma considered for some little time how to introduce so many *thats*, and at length said, "Fetch me the nosegay *that* I gathered this morning, *that* I may put it into *that* flowerpot."

"The first *that*," said Mary, "is a relative pronoun; and points to the nosegay, which is its antecedent. The second *that* is a conjunction, which joins the two parts of the sentence together; and the last *that* is a demonstrative pronoun, pointing out the particular flower-pot you want."

"I must say you have explained it very well," said her mother. "To conclude the pronouns, I must tell you that there are two other classes, called the Distributive and the Indefinite. The distributive pronoun divides a noun of multitude into parts; there are only four of this description, *every*, *each*, *either*, and *neither*. Thus you say, *every* sailor of the ship's crew; *each* member of Parliament; *either* of the pair of gloves; *neither* of the twins."

"Oh yes!" said Mary, "it takes the noun of multitude to pieces and speaks of only one part of it. But pray what are the indefinite pronouns? are they like the indefinite article?"

"Yes; for they point out a noun generally without mentioning any one in particular; as, *some* men, *all* people, *any* thing, *other* persons, *one* child, *both* sides."

"Yes," said Mary, "I like *some* books, but not *others*, but Charles is so fond of reading that he likes *all* books. But," continued she, "*one* child, and *both* sides seem to me to point out more than an indefinite pronoun should do; for when you say *one* child you mean one particular child; and *both* sides means two particular parts of something."

"That does not necessarily follow," observed her mother; "you may say, A crowd of children were at play; *one* child came up to me; but I do not tell you which it was, for *one* merely points out that it was one of the crowd. Then with regard to *both* sides, you may say, I like to see sofas on *both* sides of a drawing-room, without specifying any particular drawing-room."

Mary then asked whether all the numbers were pronouns, as well as number *one*.

"Yes," replied her mother, "as one man, two horses, three cats, four mice, and so on."

"Before we finish the pronouns," continued she, "I should tell you that several of their classes are called, by some grammarians, *adjective pronouns*, because they are placed before nouns as adjectives are. The personal pronouns in the possessive case are of this description, as, *his* hat, *your* book, *her* house, *their* pens."

"Well then," said Mary, "the four demonstrative

pronouns must be adjective pronouns also, for we say *that* boy, *this* top, *those* dolls, *these* hoops."

"The distributive and indefinite pronouns also come under this denomination by those who adopt it," continued her mother, "for you say, *each* sheep of the flock, *both* men, *all* copies, *two* pens."

"Well," said Mary, "after all I do not think these pronouns deserve the title of adjectives, for though they stand before a noun, they do not point out any of its qualities. The articles *a* and *the* might as well be called adjectives, because they stand before nouns."

"These pronouns," said her mother, "point out something relative to the noun, which more nearly resembles an adjective than the articles do. Those in the possessive case denote possession of the noun, as, *my* gown.

"The demonstrative point out the particular noun, as, *that* book.

"The distributive mark out a particular part of the noun of multitude, as, *every* cow of the drove.

"The indefinite, it is true, speak of nouns generally, but they distinctly specify the noun, as, *some* people, *other* places, *all* persons, and so forth. But I agree with you that these pronouns have not a sufficient claim to the title of adjective pronouns. We will now take leave of the pronouns."

"But don't forget, mamma, that you promised me a story after the pronouns."

To keep her promise, her mother began as follows:—

A STORY

CURIOSITY

ELLEN FORRESTER was a little girl of an amiable disposition; but she had one fault which was likely to spoil all her good qualities; this was curiosity. She was so eager to know whatever happened to her friends, that she wearied them by her questions. If she thought they talked lower than usual she contrived to get within hearing, and listened attentively to know if they were not whispering secrets; thus she was beginning to be considered as an inquisitive and prying girl, and to be avoided by her companions. She was once or twice found secretly listening, and was obliged to make some awkward excuse; but she had never gone so far as to be guilty of a direct falsehood. Her mother, who loved her tenderly, had tried various modes of curing her of this fault but without success. One day she sent her into her room to fetch some work, and Ellen saw a letter lying on the table. She felt a strong desire to look at the direction; it was in her grandmamma's hand-writing. "I wonder," thought Ellen, "mamma did not tell me of it; there is some secret in it, I dare say." This increased her curiosity. She turned the letter over, and saw that the seal was broken, and that the letter, though folded, was

226

not closed; so that, in turning it over in every direction, it became unfolded, and her own name caught her eye. She was now convinced that the letter contained a secret about herself, and her curiosity was more and more excited. She knew it would be very wrong to read the letter, yet she still kept it in her hands; and without, as she persuaded herself, intending to read it she could not avoid seeing these words, "you will give it to Ellen only, if—" she could see no more without decidedly opening the letter. What could it be that her grandmamma was going to give her; her desire to know was almost irresistible; and then the terrible *if* increased it so much, that she lost all control over herself, tore open the letter, and read as follows:—"I send a painting-box as a new-year's gift to my dear Ellen. I know she has long wished to have one, and she has made such progress in drawing that I think she will soon be able to colour her sketches; but, as I consider it of much greater importance that she should improve in character than in drawing, I beg that you will give it to Ellen only if, during a whole month previous to new-year's day, her curiosity has not led her into the commission of any fault." "No, not one!" cried Ellen, her eyes sparkling with joy; "it was but yesterday mamma said I had been good for a whole month:" but soon the conscious colour rushed to her cheeks, the letter dropped from her hands; she knew that opening it was a fault by which the present would be forfeited. What was to be done? She bitterly repented of her curiosity; but it still prevailed, and she could not help looking round the room to see if she could discover the box. There was something on the dressing-table covered with a handkerchief; she lifted it up, and beheld the painting-box, beautifully inlaid, and of a much larger size than she had expected; she raised the lid, and beneath it lay all the gay colours in soft gradation of tints, and beside them a number of camel-hair brushes of various sizes. She opened a drawer beneath, and saw a set of small saucers placed in rows, and intended for the colours when rubbed up. She was at first so much taken up with the box that she forgot her fault; but, as soon as reflection returned, she trembled with apprehension. "Alas! what can I do?" thought she; "how can I conceal my fault from my dear mamma, to whom I tell every thing? and how could I enjoy this present if she gave it to me after what I have done?" She was thus hesitating when her mother called to her from below, and asked her why she did not come back with the work she had sent her for. Ellen shut the box hastily, threw the handkerchief over it, folded up the letter, and ran down stairs so fast that she had well nigh fallen: this, she thought, might account for her agitation and confusion; but her mother was too clear-sighted; she knew by Ellen's conscious look that she had seen the box and read the letter. Her heart sunk within her through grief at her daughter's misconduct; but she said nothing, thinking it right to consider how she should act, and willing to allow her time and opportunity to make a confession. The morning passed away almost in silence; the lessons were very imperfectly learned; there were several mistakes in her reading, and her work was hemmed on the wrong side. Ellen was evidently very unhappy; and over and over again did she resolve to get rid of her curiosity; she could not have had a more favourable opportunity, had she but fortitude to sacrifice her new-year's gift and confess her fault; but her eyes had dwelt with such delight on the beauties of the box, and the possession of it appeared to her such supreme happiness, that she had not the courage to give it up. "Oh! why did my hateful curiosity make me uncover it?" said she to herself; "if I had not seen it, I should not feel so sorry to give it up: oh! why did I read the letter? it was *that* which did all the harm!" She was still hesitating what to do when, three days after, on coming into her mother's room, her mother kissed her, and wished her a happy new year. Ellen was not aware that the new year was so near at hand; she blushed and knew not what to say; her colour rose still higher, when her mother showed her the box, told her the conditions on which it was given, and then continued, in a serious and impressive manner, but with a look of anxious tenderness, as if she were entreating rather than inquiring, "I hope I can have sufficient confidence in you, my dear Ellen, to make you the judge of your own conduct: tell me whether you deserve this box or not?" Ellen could not resist this appeal; she was touched by the confidence her mother placed in her, and her beseeching look went straight to her heart. She sunk on her knees, hid her face in her mother's lap, and sobbed out, "Oh, no! no! I do not deserve it." Her mother raised her up, and embraced her with eagerness, while her eyes sparkled with joy. "My dear child," said she, "you have relieved me from a dreadful apprehension; I know your fault; you have been guilty of concealing it for three days; and if in the end you had denied it, I should have been wretched; for I should have been convinced that your insatiable curiosity had destroyed the natural candour and openness of your disposition. But you have in part atoned for your fault by your free confession; and the sacrifice of the box will, I hope, make a lasting impression on your mind." Ellen, overcome by her emotion, cried out, "Oh, mamma! I do not care for the box now, I only care for your forgiveness, and am so sorry to have made you unhappy; but I did not think you knew any thing about it." "You cannot read my countenance as well as I can yours," replied her mother; "or rather you do not observe it. I am sure, you have not seen me smile these last three days; as for you, I was aware of what you had done the moment you returned with the work." She then took Ellen out walking to compose her spirits; and, when they returned, she said, "Now let us pack up this unfortunate box, and return it to grandmamma, and I will write her word of what has happened; we must have no concealment from her." Ellen fetched the paper and packthread; she could not give a last look at the beautiful colours without some feeling of regret; but the more she suffered by parting with the box, the more she felt assured that she should in future not give way to her curiosity. As she tied the last knot, she said, "I hope it will not always be an unfortunate box; for I do think it will cure me for ever." "I wish it may," replied her mother; "and, if so, we may, perhaps, some day or other, see it back again."

LESSON XXX

VERBS—INFINITIVE MODE

"In our former lesson on verbs, when you were a little girl, Mary," said her mother, "I taught you the meaning of a verb generally, and explained to you the three kinds of verbs, *active*, *passive*, and *neuter*. Now that you are a great girl, comparatively speaking," said she, smiling, "I must teach you something more of these very important parts of speech."

"You have already told me a good deal more about verbs," replied Mary; "how they despotically govern nouns, obliging the poor nouns to be in the nominative or the objective case, just as they please to determine."

"But you have still to learn, my dear, the four different modes or the manner of expressing a verb."

"Modes of expressing a verb!" repeated Mary; "I cannot understand that without an explanation, mamma."

"Then I will endeavour to explain them to you, but we will not begin with a definition."

"I am very glad of that," said Mary; "for there is nothing so dry and hard to understand as a definition:

I think it should always come in at the end instead of the beginning."

"That is true," said her mother; "for it is then not only more easy to understand, but you naturally take more interest in a subject of which you have acquired some knowledge."

"You know, mamma, how difficult all those definitions of the parts of speech in the grammar seemed to me, until you had explained them?"

"Yes," replied her mother, "it was that which at first gave you such a dislike to grammar. Well, now, let us try to make some acquaintance with these different modes of the verb. The pronouns you have lately been learning are a very good introduction to the verbs; for without the help of persons we could not understand a verb. If I say, to write, to walk, to be beaten, you know the meaning of the verb; but you cannot tell who it is that writes, or walks, or is beaten; you are ignorant whether it is one person or many, and whether the person is masculine or feminine ——"

"Or neuter, perhaps, mamma," interrupted Mary; "for you know a pen may write, and a carpet may be beaten."

"Very true, my dear; you see, therefore, that either nouns, or personal pronouns, are necessary to tell us who it is that acts. The mere name of the verb, with the little word *to* before it, is called the *infinitive mode* of the verb, because it defines nothing, and simply expresses the action, without saying who did it, or when or how it was done; as, to sleep, to talk, to be tired."

232

"Then I think, mamma, the infinitive mode seems to teach one nothing at all."

"It teaches you little more than the name of the verb," replied her mother; "but you will find, by and by, that it is more useful than you imagine."

"Well: if, instead of saying *to write*, you say *he writes*, what does that mean?"

"I know," said Mary, "that *he* is a single person of the masculine gender, and that *he* is the person who writes; so the little word *he* points out the person, the number, and the gender. Oh, *he* tells us a great deal more than *to* does."

"It tells us something very different, at all events," replied her mother; "but does not *he* point out the case also?"

"Yes; *he* is the nominative case; for *he* does something, he writes; *he* comes before the verb, which commands it to be nominative."

"And does not *he* writes tell you also the time at which he writes?" inquired her mother.

"What do you mean, mamma?" cried Mary, looking surprised,—"at what o'clock he writes?"

"Oh no. Time in grammar, my dear," said her mother, smiling, "does not mean the hour, the day, or the year. He writes, means that he is writing now at this present time, whether it is twelve o'clock, or three o'clock, or whatever the hour may be."

"Yes, to be sure," said Mary: "or whatever day, Sunday,

Monday, or Tuesday, or whatever year it may happen to be, *he writes* means always *now*. How much more the little word *he* tells us than the little word *to* does; for it tells us the person, the number, the gender, the case, and the time."

"The word *he*, Mary, does not point out the time."

"Why, mamma, you have just said that *he writes* is *now*, the present time."

"That is true; *he writes* is the present time; but it is the word *writes*, and not the word *he*, that points out the time. The pronoun *he* is used in all the times. If I say, *he wrote* a letter yesterday, what time is that?"

"That is the time that is past and gone; for yesterday is over, and will never come back again."

"But you see, Mary, that it is the change in the verb, from *writes* to *wrote*, and not the pronoun *he*, which points out the past time. And if I say, he *shall write* to-morrow, what does that mean?"

"Oh! to-morrow is not past and gone," said Mary; "it is the time that is to come; it will be here soon, mamma."

"Very well; you must remember these three times, which grammarians call tenses; they are—

The present time, which is now;

The past time which is gone by; and

The future time, which is to come.

I ride to-day, that is the present time;

I rode yesterday, that is the past; and

I shall ride to-morrow, that is the future."

"But you say ride for the present and for the future, too, mamma, when you say I shall ride."

"The verb ride does not change," replied her mother, "it is the word *shall* which points out the future tense. *Shall* is the sign of the future tense, just as *to* is the sign of the infinitive mode."

"So, then, if you said I shall ride next week, or next year, it is the time to come, as well as to-morrow, is it not?"

"Certainly; I mentioned to-morrow only, because I thought it would make the sense clearer to you to point out some particular time.

"Well, my dear, I think you may now take a little rest, and we will reserve what we have to say on this mode till our lesson to-morrow."

"Mamma," replied Mary, "that is present time and future time; have you nothing to say on past time?"

"The lesson I have just given you is now past," said her mother, "and so good-by."

LESSON XXXI

VERBS—INDICATIVE MODE

MARY's mother inquired at the next lesson what she remembered of the mode they had been talking of so much in the last lesson.

"Oh I know a great deal about it," answered Mary; "this mode has all the three persons, both singular and plural, and the three tenses; and I like it much better than the infinitive mode; pray what is it called?"

"It is called the *indicative* mode, because it *indicates*, that is, points out that the verb is positively done, without any condition, hesitation, or objection. Now let me hear whether you can repeat the three tenses or times of the indicative mode, in the verb to walk; but use the pronoun *I* instead of *he*."

Mary looked grave; and after a little thought, said, "I walk, that is now; I walked, that means the past time; and I shall walk, that is the future."

"Very well, Mary; but *I* and *he* are not the only persons who can walk. In our lesson on pronouns, you may remember, we said, there were three persons singular and as many plural; and each of these persons

236

may be the nominative, or agent of the verb, as well as *he* or *I.*"

"Oh, yes; all the persons can not only walk, but they can run and dance too," said Mary, beginning to skip about.

"Well, when you have finished dancing yourself," said her mother, "suppose that you were to try to repeat the verb to dance; begin with the first person *I*, and go on with those that follow."

This seemed to Mary a difficult task, and one that required a good deal of reflection: so she sat down, and took some little time to think and recollect who the several pronouns were, and then said,—"I dance, you dance, he dance; no, it must be he dances," said she, interrupting herself.

"Yes," replied her mother, "the third person singular is *dances.*"

"Or, if it is a woman, or a little girl," said Mary, "it is *she* dances."

"Or, if it is a doll or a puppet," added her mamma, "it is *it* dances; and all three are the third person singular. But remember I told you that *thou* continues to be used by grammarians for the second person singular; though, in conversation and in writing, we say *you* in its stead. Now for the plural."

Mary repeated, "We dance, you dance, they dance."

"Very well: that is all the present time."

"But, mamma, if I say I am dancing, that must be present time, as well as I dance, for they both mean *now.*"

"Certainly," said her mother; "when you repeat the verb you may say, I dance or am dancing, thou dancest or art dancing, etc.: now can you tell me the past time?"

"I must think of some past time," said Mary. "Suppose it was yesterday;" she then continued, "I danced yesterday, thou dancedst yesterday, he danced yesterday; we danced, you danced, they danced. I mean that they all danced yesterday, mamma; but there is no use in repeating it every time. You see that I did not forget to say *thou* instead of *you,* for the second person singular; and then I was forced to say dance*dst,* else it would not have sounded right."

"Very well," said her mother, "and you may in the past time say, I danced or was dancing, thou dancedst or wast dancing. Now for the future, or time to come."

"Oh! that will be very easy," said Mary; "for I know the sign of the future is *shall;* so I have only to put shall before dance, and go on as I did with the past time."

"But take care, Mary," said her mother, smiling, "not to put the word 'yesterday' after the verb, as you did in the past tense."

"No, indeed; it would be foolish to say, I shall dance yesterday! Let me see! what future time shall I choose? it shall be 'to-morrow.'"

Then she repeated, "I shall dance to-morrow,

thou shalt dance to-morrow, he shall dance, we shall dance, you shall dance, they shall dance, all of them to-morrow."

"Very well, my dear," said her mother; "but I must tell you that there are *two* words which are both signs of the future tense, *shall* and *will*; if you say I will dance, it means that you are to dance at some future time also."

"Then, *shall* and *will* mean the same thing, mamma."

"As signs of the future tense they do; but their meaning is very different in other respects, according as they are placed in the sentence. Of this I will give you an amusing example:—

"There was a foreigner once in this country, who fell into a river, and not knowing how to swim, he was sadly afraid of being drowned. In his distress he called out, 'I *will* be drowned, and nobody *shall* come and help me.' Some country people who were at work in an adjoining field thought it was a joke and began to laugh; but finding by his struggles that he was really in want of assistance, they went and got him out of the water; and on coming to an explanation, they found that he had intended to call for help, and to say, 'I *shall* be drowned, and nobody *will* come and help me.'"

After Mary had laughed heartily at this anecdote, her mother said she had learnt enough of verbs this morning. She desired her to endeavour to remember the three tenses of the indicative mode, promising at their next lesson to teach her another mode.

LESSON XXXII

VERBS—SUBJUNCTIVE MODE AND IMPERATIVE MODE

"WELL, mamma," said Mary, "I cannot think what the other modes can be, besides the infinitive, which tells you so little; and the indicative, which tells you so much; in short, it seems to tell you every thing, for it does the verb in all its tenses, and all its persons, so I cannot understand how there can be any other mode of doing a verb, mamma; for either the verb must be positively done, or not done; you cannot do it by halves, can you?"

"I have known people, Mary, who cannot always make up their mind, whether they will do a verb or not. For instance, this morning when Willy was asking you to go and play with him in the garden, you answered, 'If I go, I shall not have time to finish my work;' and then, when he continued pressing you to go, you said, 'I would go if *you would* promise not to keep me long; and he having agreed to this condition, you said, 'Well, then, mamma, *may* we go?' "

"Oh, but, that was talking about doing the verb, and not positively doing it."

240

"True," replied her mother, "that was not the indicative mode."

"But you know, mamma, I did go with Willy at last; for when you said yes, I put by my work, and went directly; that was the indicative or positive mode. And is talking about whether you will do a verb or not, another mode, mamma?"

"Yes, it is called the *Subjunctive*, because some circumstance or condition is *subjoined* to it. I will give you an example; for instance, 'If you ride, the horse may throw you.' The *condition subjoined* to your riding is, that the horse *might* throw you; that is not a very agreeable circumstance."

"No, indeed," said Mary.

"Or you might say," continued her mother, "If I were to ride, I should be tired."

"That is not quite so alarming a condition," said Mary; "well, pray go on with your conditions, mamma."

Her mother went on. "If he ride, he will be too late for dinner. If we ride, it must be early. If you ride, you may get wet. If they had ridden, they might have enjoyed the fine weather."

"Well," observed Mary, "I am glad to hear there is a pleasant circumstance subjoined at last."

"The little verbs *may, might, should, would, could,*" her mother said, "are all signs of the subjunctive mode; for they all express uncertainty, and require an *if* before them; as, 'If I may ride, will you lend me your horse?' 'If he knew how to ride, he would not have been thrown;' 'If they should go, they would not be home in time.' "

"Oh, mamma!" exclaimed Mary, "that was the mode in which I was talking to Willy, about going to play with him in the garden. I remember I said, if I *should* go, and if I *may* go, and all the little hesitating verbs."

"And then you know, Mary, you made your condition that he *should* not detain you long."

"So I did," replied Mary, looking surprised. "Well, how could I talk so much in the subjunctive mode without knowing a word about it?"

"Observe, Mary," said her mother, "that in this mode the agents do not say that they do ride, or have ridden, or will ride, as they do in the indicative mode: but that they *might*, or *could*, or *would*, or *may*, under such or such conditions."

"Yes, mamma; though they talk so much about it, there is not one of them that does ride. I like the indicative mode much the best, for there you positively do ride, or have ridden, or shall ride, without so many *ifs* to stop you."

"Now, then, you understand the difference between the indicative and the subjunctive modes," said her mother.

"Oh yes; in the indicative, each of the persons ride, without any condition, or any body trying to prevent them, while the subjunctive is all made up of hesitation and uncertainty."

"Yes," said her mother, "the indicative is the *positive* mode; the subjunctive the *conditional* mode."

"I know what I should call it, mamma; I think it is the uncertain or doubting mode, for they can none of them make up their minds whether they will ride or not."

"Yet you should not find fault with their hesitation," said her mother; "for their doing the verb or not depends often on other people or circumstances, rather than on themselves."

"Then I suppose," said Mary, laughing, "the persons in the subjunctive mode are children, who can only do what they are allowed; and then you know, mamma, it is no wonder there should be so many conditions as to their riding."

"The subjunctive mode," her mother said, "applies quite as much to grown people as to children. A man may say, 'If you *would* choose me for your king, I *would* govern you with wisdom and justice.' Or a general may say to his soldiers, 'If you *should* disobey my orders, you *would* be severely punished.'"

"Or, mamma, you might say to me, 'If you *were* a good girl for a week to come, I *should* be very much pleased.' But the little word if, mamma, is not a verb, is it?"

"No; it is a conjunction which expresses doubt or uncertainty; other conjunctions are sometimes used in the subjunctive mode, as *though* and *that*. Thus you would say, '*Though* he should speak the truth, they would not believe him;' 'I wish you would lend me a book, *that* I might read.' The subjunctive mode may indeed be used without any sign; you may always know it to be subjunctive when the verb is not positive, but conditional or depending on some other circumstance.

"I will give you the subjunctive mode of the verb to dance."

I may, or might, or should,
   would, or could dance,   if you would let me.

Thou mayest, or might, or should,
   would, or could dance,   "

He may, or might, or should,
   would, or could dance,   "

We may, or might, or should,
   would, or could dance,   "

You may, or might, or should,
   would, or could dance,   "

They may, or might, or should,
   would, or could dance,   "

"Or *if* any thing else," said Mary; "as, 'If I choose,' or 'If I go to the ball,' or 'If I have a partner.' "

"Well, Mary, I think we have enough of the *ifs* now; so let us proceed to the last mode, which is called the imperative; it commands and forbids, as, '*Come* here,' '*Learn* your lesson,' '*Go away.*' "

"Oh, what a tone of authority this mode has!" said Mary.

"You need not be in great awe of it, however; for besides commanding, it also begs and entreats. Beggars speak in this mode when they say, '*Pray*, give me a halfpenny;' and children, when they ask pardon and say, '*Forgive* me.'"

"What a strange mode!" cried Mary; "at one time to order and command, and at another to beg and pray. But, mamma, are there no persons in this mode, no pronouns?"

"Oh yes," returned her mother; "the same as in the other modes. This is the imperative mode—

Let me dance,	Let us dance,
Dance thou,	Dance you,
Let him dance,	Let them dance."

"How odd!" said Mary, "*dance thou!* and *dance you!* People never say so in talking, mamma?"

"No," replied she. "It is used only in religious books or poetry, when the language is very elevated. In familiar speaking or writing, you say, *dance, write, speak.*"

"But then how is it known which of the three persons is meant?"

"The person who speaks, is, you know, always the first person, and the person spoken to the second.

When you say *dance*, you speak to the person whom you bid to dance: the pronoun *you*, therefore, though not mentioned, is understood, and it is only in the second persons, both singular and plural, that the pronoun is not used."

"It was your saying 'Come here, give me a halfpenny,' without using any pronoun, that made me think there were no persons to this mode."

"It is curious," said her mother, "that illiterate people speak most grammatically in this mode; for they say, 'Come *you* here, get *you* gone.' They learn grammar by the ear, and make the verbs more regular than they really are."

LESSON XXXIII

VERBS—SUMMARY OF MODES

At the next lesson, Mary's mother said, "I have now explained to you the four modes of the verb, and as it is very essential that you should remember them well, I wish you would repeat to me their names and their meaning."

Mary looked very grave to show that she was very attentive, and after a little reflection began thus:—

"First comes the infinitive mode, which means nothing at all except the name of the verb, with the little word *to* before it, as, 'To speak, to write.'"

"But, Mary," observed her mother, "if it is a very desirable thing to have a mode which points out so much as the indicative mode does, it is also very convenient to have a mode which expresses only the name of the verb. If I say, '*Sophy will learn to read,*' there are in that sentence two verbs, *learn* and *read.* The first is in the indicative mode, '*Sophy will learn;*' the nominative *Sophy* is of the third person, singular number, feminine gender; and *will* learn marks the future tense."

"Oh, how much is said in those three little words!" exclaimed Mary.

"Well, now tell me who is it that will read."

"Why, Sophy, to be sure, mamma."

"The sentence," replied her mother, "says, 'Sophy will learn,' but it does not say that 'Sophy will read.' "

"No, because that is not necessary. When you say, 'Sophy will learn to read,' it means that Sophy will do both the verbs learn and read."

"Since we know that it is the same person who will both *learn* and *read*, it would be a loss of time and of words to point out all these circumstances over again. To save this trouble of repetition, the second verb, therefore, is in the infinitive mode, which simply names the verb, that being all that is required. So you see, Mary, that when there are two verbs with the same nominative, it is very convenient to have so short a mode of expressing the second verb as the infinitive is."

"It is, indeed," said Mary; "I will try to find out two verbs with the same nominative."

"You have done it already, my dear; *try to find* are two verbs, the first in the indicative, the second in the infinitive mode."

"That was found out by chance," said Mary; "but now I will find out one by thinking:" and after a little reflection, she said, "I should like to eat."

"Observe, Mary," said her mother, *"I should like* is not the indicative but the subjunctive mode; but the infinitive mode follows the subjunctive mode equally as well as it does the indicative."

"But that little word *to* puzzles me, mamma; it is a preposition, not a verb, and yet it is a sign of the infinitive mode."

"When it is used as the sign of the infinitive mode," replied her mother, "you must consider it as forming part of the verb; for it is not used in the sense of the preposition before the noun. When you say *to* a house, or *to* a man, it means approaching or going *to* a house, or a man; but when *to* is used as the sign of the infinitive mode, as 'to write, to read, to dance,' it means doing something, not approaching any thing."

"Now, tell me what is the next mode?"

"The indicative," said Mary; "which is the wisest, and means the most of them all; for it speaks positively, and without hesitation; then it has the three tenses, and the three personal pronouns, both singular and plural; in short, in that mode the verb is done completely."

"Then follows the subjunctive mode, or, as I call it, the doubting mode, which has all the persons the same as the indicative mode; but they do not get on half so well; they each declare they would do the verb, if they could, or would, or might,—it is always future time with them, I think, mamma," continued Mary, laughing; "for as they never do the verb, there is no present time; and as they never did the verb, there can be no past time either."

"Grammarians, however, contrive," said her mother,

"to make out both a past and a present time in this mode; but it is not necessary to trouble you about them at present."

"Well," said Mary, "the last is the imperative mode, which is sometimes so haughty and commanding, and at others so humble."

"You have described the modes in your own way, Mary," said her mother, "which, though not very elegant, or perhaps very accurate, shows me that you understand them pretty well.

"In speaking or writing, you must always take care that the verb agrees with the noun or pronoun, in person and number, and not say, as some illiterate people do, 'I *likes* fruit;' 'They *lives* in London.'"

"Oh no, mamma; I knew that, before I learned grammar, by the sound; but now, I know the reason of it. It is not the first person singular but the third person, that ends in *s*,—he likes, and he lives."

"There is much more correct language," said her mother, "acquired by the ear than we are aware of: but you see it will not do to trust to the ear alone; without a knowledge of grammar, we are always liable to fall into mistakes."

"I think it a very natural mistake," observed Mary, "to say *they lives*, because *they* is plural, and as nouns plural commonly end in *s*, ignorant people suppose that verbs do so too."

"True," replied her mother, "but this is no apology for *I likes*, for no one can suppose the pronoun *I* to be plural. Verbs," continued she, in conclusion, "are often made up or compounded of a verb and a preposition, as *up-hold, under-stand, under-take, for-give, over-reach,* and many others."

LESSON XXXIV

VERBS—PARTICIPLES

THE following morning, when Mary went to her mother for her lesson, she said, "Well, mamma, we have not done with the verbs yet, have we?"

"Oh no," replied her mother; "far from it. Besides the four modes, there belong to a verb two words called *Participles*, because they *partake* of two parts of speech, the verb and the adjective."

"Well! that is strange," said Mary; "adjectives and verbs are such different things."

"Neither adjectives nor verbs are things," observed her mother, "for the one expresses the quality, the other an action."

"But, mamma, what can be more unlike than qualities and actions?"

"You will understand the participle better, Mary, when I have explained it to you. In order to form a participle, you have only to add the syllable *ing* or *ed* to the verb; thus *ing* added to the verb love makes the participle *loving*, and *ed* in the same manner makes the participle *loved*."

"Those words," said Mary, "are just like verbs, for they show you the action which is doing or done; but I cannot see in what they resemble an adjective."

"Did you never hear of a loving child?"

"Oh yes! and in that sense certainly loving shows the quality of the child, and is used as an adjective. Then there is a cry*ing* child, a danc*ing* bear, a sing*ing* bird; all these are qualities, no doubt."

"Well then," said her mother, "now give me some examples of the participle ending in *ed*, when used as an adjective."

This appeared to Mary more difficult, till her mother gave her the example of a learn*ed* man. She then went on with a string of them, a tir*ed* horse, a bak*ed* cake, a heat*ed* oven, a roast*ed* fowl. "Now," added she, "I see clearly how the participle answers the purpose, either of verb or adjective; so it may very justly be said to partake of both."

"Yes," replied her mother, "a participle is like a verb when it relates to an action, and like an adjective when it relates to a noun."

"But it cannot be used in both senses at the same time," said Mary.

"No, certainly," replied her mother. "When the participle ending in *ing* is used as a verb it expresses that the action is doing, or about to be done, but not finished; as, I am writ*ing*, you are sing*ing* this morning, we shall be rid*ing* out this evening. When, on the contrary, the participle ends in *ed*, it shows that the action is finished; as, the cake is spoil*ed*, the water has boil*ed*, the dog bark*ed* all night. These two participles, when thus partaking of the verb, are distinguished by the names of the *active* and the *passive* participles."

"Oh yes," said Mary, "the active participle is while the action is doing; as, talking, walking, smiling, frowning: and the passive participle when it is done; as, talk*ed*, walk*ed*, smil*ed*, frown*ed*. But I think, mamma, they might equally be called the present and the past participles; the present ending in *ing*, and the past in *ed*; for it is always present time while the action is doing, and past after it is done."

"They are also so distinguished," replied her mother; "and they are moreover sometimes called the imperfect and the perfect participles,—imperfect before the action is completed, and perfect after it is finished; thus, danc*ing* is the imperfect, and danc*ed* the perfect participle."

"You must observe," continued her mother, "that when the participle expresses the quality of a noun, it has not precisely the same meaning as a quality expressed by an adjective. The adjective simply points out the quality of the noun; as, a *little* child, a *brown* loaf, a *long* cord; but the participle does something more, for it expresses a quality which the object has acquired by some action having been done to it; as, a spoiled child, a baked loaf, a twisted cord, and points out the state of the child, the loaf, and the cord, after they have undergone the process of spoiling, baking, and twisting."

"Yes," said Mary, "the participles give you to understand that the child has become disagreeable from being spoiled, the loaf eatable from being baked, and the cord strong from being twisted."

"That," replied her mother, "is the inference which the mind draws, though the participle does not actually express it."

"But," said Mary, "when these participles are used as verbs, how can you put pronouns before them? You cannot say, 'I dancing, he dancing; they dancing."

"No, when the participle is used as a verb, you require the help of another verb, as you see by and by. Now try to find out some participles, Mary?"

"*Going*, and *gone*, mamma; those are the two participles of the verb to go. Well, I will now act the two participles;" and she walked towards the door.

"I suppose that means *going*, Mary?" said her mother.

"Yes, going is the active participle." She then opened the door, and, walking out of the room, said, "Now I am *gone;* that is the passive participle." Presently she came back and said, "Now I am *a coming.*"

"*A coming!*" repeated her mother; "what sort of a thing can that be?"

"It is not a thing, mamma; it is the active participle of the verb to come."

"No, Mary. What part of speech is *a?*"

Mary began repeating from her grammar, "*A* is an

article put before a noun,"—when her mother said, "If so, *coming* must be a noun; and as I never saw or heard of such a thing as *a coming*, it is very natural that I should wonder what it can be: can you tell me whether it is a person or a thing?"

Mary tried to laugh when she discovered that her mamma was joking; but she could not do it with a good grace, for she was vexed at the blunder she had made.

"Well," continued her mother, seeing Mary look grave, "we will joke no more. *Coming*, it is true, is the present participle of the verb to come; but then you must not put an article before it, Mary, or you will make me fancy it is a noun. A great many years ago, people used to put an *a* before the participle, as you did with the participle *coming;* but that mode of speaking is no longer used but by illiterate people. I am *a* coming, I burst out *a* laughing, he fell *a* crying, are all of them incorrect expressions which should be avoided. Well, now that you are acquainted with the participles and the four modes of a verb, let me hear if you can conjugate one."

"What is conjugate, mamma?"

"It is to repeat a verb through, with its persons, its tenses, its modes, and its participles."

"As we did the verb to dance?"

"Yes; but the conjugation was not complete, as you were then not acquainted with the participles. Try to repeat the verb *to go*."

Mary stood upright before her mother, and, with a look of great attention, said, "*To go.* That is the infinitive mode. Then comes the indicative, the present tense of which is,

I go	We go
Thou goest	You go
He goes	They go

Now for the past tense. I goed, thou goedst—oh, mamma," exclaimed she, "that will never do! I am sure that *goed* is wrong; what is the past tense?"

"Indeed, Mary, I shall not tell you; you must find it out yourself."

"Let me see," said Mary; "I should not say that I *goed* out yesterday, but that I *went* out yesterday; but can *went* be the past time of the verb *to go?*"

"It is, indeed."

"How very strange, mamma! *went* and *go* are not the least alike; one is as long again as the other, and they have not even a single letter the same."

"This shows," replied her mother, "that the verb is irregular; that is to say, that in its conjugation it does not follow the common rules. Now go on."

Mary went on with the past tense.

I went	We went
Thou wentest	You went
He went	They went

"Next comes the future tense; I remember the signs of it are shall or will.

I shall go	We shall go
Thou shalt go	You shall go
He shall go	They shall go

"I am quite glad to return to the verb to go."

"In the subjunctive and imperative modes," said her mother, "*go* is also used."

Mary went on:—

I may, or might, or could go	We may go
Thou mayest go	You may go
He may go	They may go

"Then the imperative mode is,

258

Let me go	Let us go
Go thou	Go you
Let him go	Let them go

"And, lastly, the participles are going and gone. I was very near saying *goed*, mamma; but I recollected just in time."

"If the verb had been regular," said her mother, "the past tense and passive participle would have been *goed*; for, in regular verbs, these are always the same, and end in *ed*. In the verb to work, for instance, the past tense is worked, and the passive participle is worked also. Can you find out any regular verb by this method?"

"I will try, mamma. Let me see if the verb to write is regular; the past is, I wrote, then it must be irregular, because it does not end in *ed*."

"Nor does the participle either," said her mother; "for the participles are *writing, written*."

"In the verb to talk," continued Mary, "the past tense is talked; now let us see what are the participles—*talking* and *talked*. That will do, mamma," cried she, quite pleased at her success; "to talk, is a regular verb. And the verb to learn must be a regular verb also, for *learned* is both the past tense and the past participle; and the verb to walk is regular also, mamma."

"Well, that will do, Mary; you have found out examples enough to make you remember the rule."

"Oh! but do let me find out a few irregular verbs." She thought a little, and then said, *"to give* is irregular; for the past is *gave*, and the participle *given*. And the verb *to feel*,—though, I do not know," added she, "for the past is *felt*, and the participle is *felt* too, so they are the same."

"But they do not end in *ed*," said her mother, "therefore it is irregular. The irregular are almost as numerous as the regular verbs. I will give you a list of some of the principal verbs, distinguishing the regular from the irregular:—

Regular Verbs

Infinitive	Past Time	Participle
To walk	I walked	walked
To love	I loved	loved
To dance	I danced	danced
To prepare	I prepared	prepared
To decide	I decided	decided
To refuse	I refused	refused
To wish	I wish	wished

Irregular Verbs

Infinitive	*Past Time*	*Participle*
To begin	I began	begun
To beseech	I besought	besought
To break	I broke	broken
To read	I read	read
To bring	I brought	brought
To lie	I lay	lain
To lose	I lost	lost
To shake	I shook	shaken
To strike	I struck	stricken
To write	I wrote	written
To sing	I sang	sung

"But we have had verbs enough for to-day, Mary; so put on your bonnet and take a run in the garden."

A STORY

THE RIVAL FRIENDS

Susan and Lucy were two friends, who went to the same school. The ladies who lived in the neighbourhood superintended the school, and three prizes were given every year. The first was for the girl who had been to school most regularly, the second for the ablest scholar, and the third for her who was the best girl of the school.

Susan stood no chance of having the first prize; for, her mother having been ill for some months past, she had often been obliged to stay at home to assist her, and to take care of the younger children. But she was so attentive to her poor sick mother, so careful of her brothers and sisters, and so kind, and good-tempered, that every one wished, and expected her to gain the third prize.

Lucy was a clever girl; she had a remarkably good memory, and she understood and took pleasure in what she learnt. She wished her friend to gain the third prize, because she loved her dearly; and she felt pretty certain of having the second herself. She was ambitious of being thought the cleverest girl in the school; and then she knew that it was more easy to out-do Susan in learning than in goodness.

At length the day of examination arrived. The children were all neatly dressed in their Sunday clothes, and accompanied by their mothers to the school. Susan was sadly grieved that her mother was too unwell to go with her. But her mother kissed her at parting, and said, "Come back, my child, with the prize you deserve, and that will do me more good than all the doctor's physic." These words pleased Susan, and made her wish more than ever to gain the prize of goodness. When the children were assembled in the school-room, they saw the three prizes hung up in full view. The first was a pretty shawl; the second, a straw bonnet, trimmed with blue ribands; and the third, a pink and white calico frock. The ladies examined the school books, and found that Eliza Hawkins had attended the greatest number of times: the first prize was therefore given to her, accompanied by a few words of praise, and she returned to her place much pleased.

The second prize was to be gained by a trial of skill. A subject was given for a theme, on which the scholars were to write. Half an hour was allowed them for the task, during which time no intercourse was permitted between the children, and they were to keep perfect silence. Susan and Lucy sat beside each other on the same form, in anxious expectation. The subject given was the discovery of America. The girls all took up their pens, and began thinking what they should write. Susan wrote all she could recollect of Columbus's voyage, across unknown seas; the danger he ran of being forced by his crew to return; of the delight he felt when he first discovered land, and the manner in which he was received by the savages of the new country.

She had got so far, when she heard her friend say in a low whisper, "What shall I do? I can't recollect the man's name; oh, Susan, help me!"

Susan was astonished; she had expected Lucy to write by far the best account of America, but poor Lucy could do nothing while her mind was bewildered by trying to recollect the name. Susan wrote on a small slip of paper *"Christopher Columbus,"* and pushed it under the long desk, on which they were writing, to her companion, who eagerly seized it, began writing with great earnestness, and went on so fast, that at the end of the half hour, not only was her theme ready, but it was decidedly the best, and the prize was given to her. One of the ladies put the bonnet on Lucy, and tied it under her chin. All the children admired the bonnet, but without envy; they thought that Lucy deserved it, and looked pleased to see how well it became her; but no one was more sincerely pleased than Susan, though she herself would have won the prize, if she had not helped Lucy; Lucy's colour rose with delight and exultation; but when she looked at Susan, and thought what she had done to help her, her eyes sparkled with gratitude; and she now more than ever hoped that the last remaining prize would be given to Susan.

The moral conduct of the several children was then inquired into; Susan was declared to be the best girl of the school, and was called up to receive the prize; but before she could reach the spot, Mrs. Moreley arose, and motioning with her hand that it should be replaced upon the table, said, "I regret to have any thing to say against so good a girl as Susan; but it is my duty to report what I observed this morning: a written paper passed between Lucy and Susan whilst they were writing the theme. They are both to blame for breaking our rules; it was, however, so kind of Lucy to assist Susan, that we must excuse her fault. But," continued she with a graver look, "unless Susan can clear herself, she cannot deserve the prize for good conduct."

Mrs. Moreley, knowing that Lucy was a better scholar than Susan, had supposed that the paper she had seen pass between them came from Lucy, instead of having been given to her.

During Mrs. Moreley's speech, Lucy's colour came and went; she breathed hard, and at length burst into tears. Susan, on the contrary, heard the accusation with composure, and determined not to disclose the truth which would deprive Lucy of her prize. She therefore looked down, but made no answer.

Susan had some hope, it is true, that Lucy would come forward and reveal the truth; but though Lucy dearly loved her friend, she had not courage to do so, as she would thus confess her own fault; she therefore grieved for her, but without speaking. Foolish girl! she little thought how much her character would have risen, if she had at once done justice to Susan; and how utterly despised she would be if the truth should be discovered in any other manner. Susan's silence was considered as an admission of her guilt, and the prize of good conduct was given to another girl.

Lucy could contain her feelings no longer; she went up to Susan, kissed her with warmth and tenderness, took the bonnet off her own head and put it on that of her friend; saying, "It is yours, Susan." But Susan would not take it. Mrs. Moreley thought that Lucy carried her grief for the disappointment of her friend too far and said to her: "Susan's fault is not great, and I regret that, occurring at this moment, it should deprive her of this prize; how much more bitter her feelings would have been, if by the assistance you gave her you had been deprived of the other!" These words, instead of consoling Lucy, did but increase her grief; for it was she who felt the bitter remorse which Mrs. Moreley spoke of. She hung upon Susan's neck in an agony of grief; Susan whispered to her, "Speak out, Lucy, and it will be all over. I say so, as much for your sake as for my own." "I cannot," replied Lucy; "I dare not face such shame; but do you speak for me;" and then dreading to hear what Susan would say, she ran out of the school-room.

Poor Susan knew not what to do. If Lucy had herself confessed the truth, it would have atoned for her conduct; but for Susan to make the disclosure, would be far from producing the same effect; besides, it might appear as if she were taking advantage of Lucy's absence, to clear herself at the expense of her friend. She determined, therefore, to say nothing; and, distressed by the look of wonder and disappointment which was fixed on her by all present, she begged leave to go home.

Her tears, which she had hitherto restrained, fell in abundance when she beheld her mother's pale countenance, and knew that she brought back nothing to cheer her. But no sooner had she told all that had passed, than her mother's anxious look was changed into a happy smile. She kissed Susan, and said that she doubly deserved the prize, and that was better than bringing it home. "Besides," added she, "I am sure that when Lucy knows that you have not spoken for her, she will speak out for herself." "Oh! but you will keep my secret, dear mother?" said Susan. "Yes," replied her mother, "whatever you confide to me, I never disclose." Susan's mother was right in her conjecture; as they were sitting in the porch of the farm-house in the evening, they saw Lucy and her mother approach. Lucy had persuaded her mother not to go till it was nearly dark, that her shame might be less observed; and even then she slunk behind her as they drew near the house. "Lucy is come," said her mother, "to ask Susan's forgiveness, and to learn what passed at the school when her fault was known." "Her fault is not known," said Susan; "I could not betray her." Lucy felt all Susan's kindness, but she dreaded the thoughts of having to make the confession herself. Her mother insisted on its being done publicly. "All those," said she, "who saw her false glory must see her shame; it is the only way she can atone for her conduct." The next day at the meeting of the Sunday school before church, Lucy told every thing that had passed. Susan looked so bashful, that you might almost have supposed it was she who had done wrong; while Lucy gained courage as she saw the pleasure that

Susan's vindication gave to every one. But if the one friend rose higher than ever in the good opinion of all, the other regained their confidence by the frankness of her confession; and, instead of feeling the shame and confusion which she expected, she found her mind relieved from a heavy weight. The little girl who had received the prize of good conduct now came up and put it into Susan's hand, but Susan would not take it, and Mrs. Moreley desired the child to keep it, saying, "Susan has gained the affection and approbation of every one; she wants no other reward." "Oh, but she must have the straw bonnet," said Lucy, with earnestness, "indeed, indeed, she must," and she put it on her head, and tied it so tight that Susan could not undo the knot. Susan looked distressed; but Mrs. Moreley said, "You cannot, my dear, refuse to give Lucy the pleasure of seeing you wear it."

LESSON XXXV

AUXILIARY VERBS

"THERE are several little verbs which are called auxiliary verbs, or helping verbs, because they assist us in the conjugation of other verbs."

"Do you mean the little verbs may, might, should, would, could, which are so much used in the subjunctive mode?" said Mary.

"Yes," replied her mother; "and also the verbs *shall* and *will*, which you know are used in the future tense; and *let*, which is the sign of the imperative mode; in short, whenever a verb helps you to conjugate another verb it is called an auxiliary verb, because auxiliary means to help."

"And what are the other verbs called, mamma?"

"They are distinguished by the name of principal verbs."

"Well they deserve that title," said Mary: "for they are of much more consequence than the little bits of helping verbs."

"There are, however," replied her mother, "two auxiliary verbs of very great importance; *to have* and *to be.* They are both so irregular, that it is necessary you should learn the conjugation of each of them by heart. Let us begin with the verb to have."

Infinitive Mode

To have

Indicative Mode

Present Time

	Singular	Plural
1st Person	I have	We have
2nd Person	Thou hast	You have
3rd Person	He, she, or it, has or hath	They have

Past Time

	Singular	Plural
1st Person	I had	We had
2nd Person	Thou hadst	You had
3rd Person	He, she, or it, had	They had

Future Time

	Singular	Plural
1st Person	I shall, or will, have	We shall, or will, have
2nd Person	Thou shalt, or wilt, have	You shall, or will, have

| 3rd
Person | He, she, or it,
shall, or will, have | They
shall, or will, have |

Subjunctive Mode

If I have, or may, might, would, could, or should, have

If thou have, or may, might, would, could, or should, have

If he, she, or it have, or may, might, would, could, or
should, have

If we have, or may, might, would, could, or should, have

If you have, or may, might, would, could, or should, have

If they have, or may, might, would, could, or should, have

Imperative Mode

1st Person	Let me have	Let us have
2nd Person	Have thou	Have you
3rd Person	Let him, her, or it, have	Let them have

Participles

| *Active* | Having |
| *Passive* | Had |

"But what does to *have* mean, mamma, all by itself, as it is in the conjugation? I can understand what to have spoken, or to have slept, or to have a cold, means; but *to have* all alone, seems nonsense."

"To have, all alone, as you call it, Mary, that is to say, when it is not followed by another verb, cannot be an auxiliary verb."

"No, to be sure," said Mary, laughing, "it cannot help to conjugate another verb, if there is no other to conjugate."

"Therefore, when the verb *to have* is conjugated by itself, it becomes a principal verb, and means possession, that is to say, that you have something."

"Then you should say what it is you *have*," said Mary, "else *have* is nonsense,—at least," added she, colouring at her own presumption, "I cannot understand it."

"Well, then, we must think of something you possess; your work-box for instance; and you may say I have a work-box."

"Yes," cried Mary, "it means something that belongs to me; something that is mine."

"Yes, but you may also possess something that does not belong to you, and is not yours. If a thief steal a purse of money, he is possessed of it, though it certainly does not belong to him."

"And when Sophy left me her doll to take care of, when she went to aunt Howard's, I had possession of it, though it did not belong to me; for you know she did not give it to me, mamma, she only lent it. I understand it very well," continued she; "*to have* means when you have something, whether it belongs to you

272

or not; as, 'I have Sophy's doll, you have a carriage, he has a horse.'"

"Yes," said her mother, "the nouns doll, carriage, and horse, are the things possessed.

"So you see that when *to have* is a principal verb, a *noun* follows to tell you what is the thing possessed. But when *to have* is used as a helping verb, instead of being followed by a noun, it is followed by *another verb*, which it helps to conjugate. Let us find some examples. I have a book which amuses me, and I have read it all through."

"I have a book," said Mary, "means that you possess the book, and *have* is there a principal verb, meaning possession—but to have read it, is quite a different thing; for here *have*, instead of being a principal verb, and possessing any thing, becomes a mere help to the verb 'to read.'"

"So you see, Mary, that in the one case something is possessed, and in the other something is done."

"Oh yes, we possess the noun, and we do the verb; that will be a good way to find out whether *have* is a principal or an auxiliary verb. When something is possessed it is a principal verb, when something is done it is an auxiliary verb. Yet, mamma, I have just thought of a sentence that puzzles me. Suppose that I say, I have bought a doll; does *have* belong to the verb bought, or to the noun doll?"

"To the verb bought," said her mother, "which immediately follows it. If you said I have a doll, then the verb to have would become a principal verb, and doll the thing possessed."

LESSON XXXVI

VERBS—TENSES

At their next lesson Mary's mother asked her, whether she could tell her what part of a principal verb was used when it is conjugated with an auxiliary verb.

"No, indeed, I do not know," replied Mary.

"It is the *participle*," rejoined her mother; "and when you say, to have spoken, to have slept, to have danced, you mention the participles of those verbs, without thinking of it."

"So I do," exclaimed Mary; "how much grammar I knew before I began to learn it, mamma!"

"I will now write down," said her mother, "the present tense of the verb *to have spoken*.

I have spoken	We have spoken
Thou hast spoken	You have spoken
He has spoken	They have spoken

"It is unnecessary for me to go on any farther, for you

have only to add the passive participle to the verb *to have*, throughout the conjugation."

"But does the participle *spoken* never change, mamma?"

"No, my dear. Why should it? the helping verb renders any change in the verb unnecessary. The auxiliary verb marks all the changes of time, as, I *have* spoken, I *had* spoken, I *shall have* spoken. So the principal verb sits at his ease, and is waited upon by the helping verb. Grammarians, by means of the verb *to have*, contrive to make out the several tenses in the conjugation of the principal verb."

"How can you make out more than three tenses?" inquired Mary; "it seems to me impossible; for you know the present tense, that is, *now*, stands in the middle, and all that goes before *now* is past time, and all that comes after *now* is future time. Yesterday, and last week, and last year, are past time; and to-morrow, and next week, and next year, are future time. How very long the past and the future time are!"

"Can you tell how long, Mary?"

"Oh no; for I do not know either when they begin or end. The past time begins, I suppose, from the beginning of the world."

"At least," said her mother, "we know nothing of the time that was before the world was made."

"Well, I think that is quite long enough," said Mary; "and then the future time, will that be to the end of the world?"

276

"Longer still," replied her mother, "for the future time will be for ever."

"So, then," said Mary, "all the time that is to come for a hundred thousand years, and more too, is future time."

"Yes, my dear, from the next minute to all eternity."

"Oh, what length of time!" exclaimed Mary.

"It is of all lengths," observed her mother; "if you say I shall go in a moment, the future time is not very long."

"No, indeed," said Mary, laughing, "a moment is short enough."

"But how odd it is, that whilst the past and the future time are so long, the present time should be so short—only just now this instant; and then," continued she after a pause, "it is gone!"

"And whither is it gone, Mary?"

"Oh, I am sure, mamma, that is more than I can tell; I only know that it is gone by and past."

"Then," said her mother, "if it is past, is it not become *past time?*"

"Ah! so it is, to be sure," said Mary, smiling at the discovery, and pleased to see that the present time, which appeared to her so short, was not lost, though it was gone.

"And is there no present time now, Mary?"

"Oh yes; *now* is always the present time, while one is saying or doing any thing."

"Then if there is always a present time," said her mother, "I should think the present time as long as either the past or the future."

"Indeed! so it is, mamma. I did not think of that; for though the present time goes away in an instant, another follows the next instant, and so it always lasts; it is made up of instants following each other."

"You know that every instant of the past time must have been present time, before it passed by and became past time? Breakfast time is now past and gone, but it was present time, this morning, while we were eating our breakfast."

"Yes," said Mary; "and last night was present time when it was dark, and I was asleep, but it is past time now that daylight is come again. Then every instant of the time to come, that is, the future time, will become present time some day or other; and then when it has passed the moment of being present time, it will become past time. I think, mamma," added she, laughing, "time goes backwards, like a crab."

Mamma laughed also at Mary's comparison. "It is true," said she, "we look forward to the future time, and when it comes up to us, and passes the moment *now*, we look back upon it as the past time."

"Well, Mary, when we began this discussion on time, I was telling you that grammarians divide the past and the future into several parts, by the help of the verb *to have*."

"And I said, mamma, that I could not understand how that could be done; for when once the time has passed, it can be no other than past time."

"Certainly; but it may be past a little while or a long while, or something may happen to interrupt you whilst you were doing the verb, and prevent your completing it. For example, you may say, *I wrote*, or *was writing*, to my brother, but Sophy came to play with me, and prevented my finishing the letter. *I wrote*, or *was writing*, is certainly past time; but as it is possible the action may not have been completed, it is called the *imperfect tense*. But if you say, *I have written* to my brother, the sense of the phrase shows that the action has been completed; this is therefore called the *perfect tense*."

"Yes," said Mary, "I understand the difference of these two past times very well."

"But that is not all," continued her mother: "suppose you were to say, *I had written* to my brother before I received his letter, what past tense would you call that, Mary?"

"Indeed, I cannot tell, mamma; for it seems more perfect than the perfect tense, as it shows that the letter had been written and finished before the other letter arrived."

"It therefore in some measure points out the period of past time," replied her mother, "and being, as you say, more perfect than the perfect tense, it is called the *pluperfect* tense."

"The future tense may be divided into parts in the same manner. I shall write, means that I intend to write some time or other, without naming the period; but if I say, I shall have written before you set out, it means that I shall write sooner than another event takes place—that is, your setting out. I will write you out a verb, with all these tenses complete, in order that you may learn them by heart."

Infinitive Mode
To talk

Indicative Mode
Present Time

	Singular	Plural
1st Person	I talk	We talk
2nd Person	Thou talkest	You talk
3rd Person	He, she, or it, talks or talketh	They talk

Past Time Imperfect

1st Person	I talked	We talked
2nd Person	Thou talkedst	You talked
3rd Person	He, she, or it, talked	They talked

Past Time Perfect

1st Person	I have talked	We have talked
2nd Person	Thou hast talked	You have talked
3rd Person	He, she, or it, has talked	They have talked

Past Time Pluperfect

1st Person	I had talked	We had talked
2nd Person	Thou hadst talked	You had talked
3rd Person	He, she, or it, had talked	They had talked

1st Future Time

1st Person	I shall, or will, talk	We shall, or will, talk
2nd Person	Thou shalt, or wilt, talk	You shall, or will, talk
3rd Person	He, she, or it, shall, or will, talk	They shall, or will, talk

2nd Future Time

1st Person	I shall have talked	We shall have talked
2nd Person	Thou shalt have talked	You shall have talked

281

3rd Person   He, she, or it, shall   They shall
              have talked   have talked

Subjunctive Mode

If I talk, or may, might, would, could, or should, talk

If thou talk, or mayest, might, would, could, or should, talk

If he, she, or it, talk, or may, might, would, could, or should, talk

If we talk, or may, might, would, could, or should, talk

If you talk, or may, might, would, could, or should, talk

If they talk, or may, might, would, could, or should, talk

Imperative Mode

	Singular	*Plural*
1st Person	Let me talk	Let us talk
2nd Person	Talk thou	Talk you
3rd Person	Let him, her, or it, talk	Let them talk

Participles

Active	Talking
Passive	Talked

LESSON XXXVII

THE VERB TO BE

"WE will begin to-day, Mary," said her mother, "with the conjugation of the verb to be."

"*To be* what, mamma?" asked Mary. "Do you mean to be pretty or ugly? to be good or naughty?"

"Yes," replied her mother; "but let us begin by conjugating the verb, I will explain its meaning afterwards."

She then went on as follows:

Infinitive Mode

To be

Indicative Mode

Present Time

	Singular	Plural
1st Person	I am	We are
2nd Person	Thou art	You are
3rd Person	He, she, or it, is	They are

Past Time

	Singular	Plural
1st Person	I was	We were
2nd Person	Thou wast	You were
3rd Person	He, she, or it, was	They were

Future Time

	Singular	Plural
1st Person	I shall, or will, be	We shall, or will, be
2nd Person	Thou shalt, or wilt, be	You shall, or will, be
3rd Person	He, she, or it, shall, or will, be	They shall, or will, be

Subjunctive Mode

Present Time

If I be, or may, might, would, could, or should, be

If thou beest, or may, might, would, could, or should, be

If he, she, or it, be, or may, might, would, could, or should, be

If we be, or may, might, would, could, or should, be

If you be, or may, might, would, could, or should, be

If they be, or may, might, would, could, or should, be

Past Time

If I were

If thou wert

If he, she, or it, were

If we were

If you were

If they were

Imperative Mode

1st Person	Let me be	Let us be
2nd Person	Be thou	Be you
3rd Person	Let him, her, or it, be	Let them be

Participles

Active	Being
Passive	Been

"What a strange verb this is!" cried Mary. "Who would ever guess that I am, thou art, he is, we are, you are, they are, was the present tense of the verb *to be?* If it were conjugated I be, thou beest, he bees, as it ought to be, there would be some sense in it."

"But the sound!" exclaimed her mother, putting her

hand to her ears. "I cannot bear the buzzing of your bees, Mary."

"Oh, you need not be frightened," returned Mary, carrying on the joke, "my bees will not sting you, mamma."

"Then the past tense," continued she, "I was, thou wast, he was, is as unlike the verb to be, as possible."

"It is very true, my dear; nothing can be more irregular than this verb; it is difficult to discover that you are conjugating the verb *to be*, till you come to the future tense, which is regular—I shall be, thou shalt be," etc.

"Then, mamma, there is a past tense in the subjunctive mode—if I were, if thou wert, if he were—quite unlike the verb to be, again!"

"But the imperative mode," said her mother, "which finishes the conjugation, is regular. If you get the verb perfectly by heart, you will no longer be perplexed with its irregularities."

"Well, this tiresome little verb to be," said Mary, "is the most difficult of all to understand. It is called a helping verb, but I think it only helps to puzzle one, for I really do not know what it means."

"*To be*, like *to have*, may be conjugated by itself, as I have just repeated it to you, and is then a principal verb. *To be* means to exist."

"But what is to exist?" inquired Mary; "is it to be alive?"

"People use the word in different significations," said her mother; "but it is enough for us to know that whatever *is* exists, whether it be alive or not. That rock lying yonder, Mary, exists, as well as you or I, though in a very different state of existence, certainly."

"Yes, indeed," cried Mary, "I should not like to exist like that great stone at all; not to be able to feel, nor to move, nor even to be moved," added she, "it is so large."

"It is true, Mary, that even in this world your existence has every advantage over that of the stone, except that it will probably last longer than you will in your present state; that rock has been there as long as I can remember, and may remain there not only during your life, but for years after."

Mary seemed rather surprised at the stone having any advantage over her, and exclaimed, "Well, but after all, there is no pleasure in existing in that manner, without feeling."

"That I grant," said her mother; "but let us return to the verb to be. If you add a noun to it, to point out the particular state of existence, it will be easier to understand. *I am* by itself is rather puzzling at your age, I must confess: but if you add the noun child, and say, I am a child, the meaning is quite clear. Thus you may say, she is a woman, he is a man, they are soldiers, we are musicians."

"Oh yes," said Mary, "the verb *to be* is easy enough to understand when a noun is added to it; and so is the verb *to have*, mamma. Don't you remember how easy it was when we added a noun to it, as, I have a horse, he has a coat? But when you say, I am a child, or you are a woman, that does not mean to possess something, as the verb *to have* does when you add a noun to it."

"No, certainly," replied her mother; "else the two verbs would have the same meaning, and one of them would be useless. The verb *to have*, when used as a principal verb, means possession; and the verb *to be*, used as a principal verb, means existence. Now, if you add a noun to the verb *to have*, it shows what it is you possess; and if you add a noun to the verb *to be*, it points out how or in what state you exist."

"That is to say, what you are," cried Mary, "whether a man, or a woman, or that stone there, mamma, that we have been talking about; only," added she, "it cannot speak and say, 'I am a stone.'"

"No, but you may speak of it in the third person, Mary, and say, 'That *is* a stone.' An adjective also frequently points out the state of existence: as, he is happy, they are wise, we are good."

"When the verb *to be* is conjugated as an auxiliary verb," said Mary, "I suppose the passive participle of the principal verb is added to it, as it is with the verb to have—Oh no, it cannot be so," said she, interrupting herself: "you cannot say I am danced, I was danced."

"*You* cannot say so, it is true, Mary; because you are rather too big to be danced in your nurse's arms; but Sophy is danced; and if she could conjugate a verb, she might say to other children of her own age, I am danced, you are danced, she is danced, we are danced, and so on."

After Mary had laughed at the idea of her little sister Sophy conjugating a verb in her nurse's arms, her mother continued:—"And which participle would you use for yourself, Mary, who can dance all alone?"

"Oh, I have found it out, mamma! it is the active participle *dancing*—I am dancing, thou art dancing, he is dancing;" and as she repeated the verb, she held out her frock and began practising the last new steps her dancing master had taught her. "Look, mamma," said she, "how clever I am, taking two lessons at once,— dancing and learning grammar."

"Well," said her mother, "you may finish your lesson in dancing, for I think you have had enough of grammar for to-day."

LESSON XXXVIII

CONSTRUCTION OF PASSIVE VERBS

"Did you observe, Mary," said her mother, "in consequence of the discovery you made at the last lesson, that you may use both the active and passive participles with the verb *to be*, while you can only use the passive with the verb to have."

"Then, mamma," said Mary, "the passive participle has two helping verbs to wait upon it, whilst the active participle has only one; that is not fair."

"Oh," said her mother, "the active participle is such a busy body, that it requires less assistance. Now, Mary, find out some examples of the verb *to be* conjugated with the active participle of the principal verb."

"I am writing, you are talking, they are fighting," said Mary.

"That will do," replied her mother; "now for some examples with the passive participle."

Mary reflected a little, and then said,—"I am forgotten, you are forgiven, it is broken."

"Very well, Mary; but these participles all belong to an irregular verb. Give me an example with a passive participle of a regular verb, which, you know, always ends in *ed.*"

Mary considered for some little time before she could think of one; then several were at once recalled to her memory, and she repeated in quick succession, "I am pleased, you are caressed, she is scolded, they are admired. But, mamma," cried she, interrupting herself, "these are all passive verbs: I remember that you explained them to me before."

"You are quite right, my dear: when I taught you the meaning of a passive verb, I said that instead of doing any thing yourself, something was done to you. This, it is true, was an explanation suited to your capacity when first you began grammar; but now that you have made some little progress in it, I may tell you that *a passive verb consists of a passive participle conjugated with the auxiliary verb to be:* this verb *to be*, you know, indicates a state of existence, and forms an essential part of a passive verb. An active verb may be conjugated without any auxiliary; or it may be conjugated with the auxiliary verb *to have*, as, I have loved; but the passive verb *cannot* be conjugated without the verb *to be*. You see, therefore, Mary, of what importance this little verb *is*, which you thought so insignificant."

"Indeed I beg its pardon," said Mary, joining her hands in an attitude of supplication; "I hope it will be pleased to forgive me."

"The passive participle *been*," continued her mother,

"may be used as a principal verb, and then it is conjugated with the auxiliary *to have;* as, I have been, thou hast been, etc."

"There is one thing which puzzles me, mamma," said Mary; "when I knock at your door in the morning, and you ask Who is there? should I answer It is *me,* or It is *I?*"

"Do you recollect," replied her mother, "that *I* is the nominative case, and *me* the objective?"

"Oh then, I should answer It is *me,* for I remember the nominative case comes before the verb, and the objective case after it, and I think *me* sounds more easy and natural."

"But unfortunately," replied her mother, "it is not the most correct, for in the verb *to be* an exception is made to this general rule, the auxiliary verb *to be* requiring the nominative case after it, as well as before it, so you should say, It is *I.*"

"Well, that is very strange," cried Mary; "but I recollect that when you explained the cases of nouns you said there were some exceptions to this rule."

"We may now," said her mother, "take leave of the verbs; but before you go, let me ask you whether you recollect the different sorts of verbs which I taught you in our first conversation upon them? What is a verb active?"

"It is a verb," answered Mary, "in which not only an action is performed, but that action must be done to some object; as, I stroke the cat, I eat an apple."

"And a passive verb?"

"It is one in which the nominative is acted upon, whilst itself remains passive; as, I am beaten."

"Recollect also," said her mother, "that both these verbs are called transitive, because the action passes over, whether it be from the agent to the object, or from the object to the agent.

"Now, tell me, what is a verb neuter?"

"It is one in which the action does not pass over to any object; and is, therefore, called intransitive, as, I sleep, I walk."

"And what is a principal verb?"

"It is one that may be conjugated without the help of an auxiliary verb."

"You are not correct there, Mary," said her mother. "You would define a principal verb more accurately, if you said that it is one which *cannot* be conjugated without the help of the auxiliary verbs *to have*, or *to be*. All principal verbs require the assistance of an auxiliary verb in their conjugation: *let*, in the imperative mode; *shall* and *will*, in the future tense; and the words used in the subjunctive mode to express uncertainty; such as, *may, should, could*, are all, strange as it may seem, auxiliary verbs.

"Now what is an auxiliary verb?"

"Any verb which assists in the conjugation of a principal verb."

"Lastly, what are participles?"

"They are two words belonging to a verb, and are called participles, because they partake of the adjective and of the verb. When used as a verb, they must be conjugated with the auxiliary verb *to have*, or *to be.*"

"I am very glad to find that you remember what you have learnt, so well: I have no further remarks to make on the other parts of speech; so, I believe, Mary, that we may now conclude our lessons, till you are old enough to learn Syntax: a branch of grammar which requires more sense and reflection than children have at your age."

"But since there are no more parts of speech to learn, mamma, what can Syntax be?"

"It teaches you," replied her mother, "how to place the several parts of speech in their proper places, when you speak or write; in short, how to speak and write correctly."

"But, mamma," said Mary, "I am sure you will not finish without a story."

"No," replied her mother; "I have prepared one for the conclusion, which I think will make you laugh."

Mary's curiosity was much excited; but she was obliged to wait till the next day, when her mother told her the following story.

A STORY

SHEEP STEALING

"A POOR labouring man was taken up for stealing sheep. He was carried before a justice, who inquired his name, and what he had to say in his defence. 'My name is Noun,' replied he; 'I am a hard-working man, and never stole a sheep or any thing else in my life.' But as the people who brought him declared that they had seen him secretly carrying away a sheep, the magistrate committed him to prison, and he was locked up in a cell, with nothing to eat but a loaf of bread, and nothing to drink but a jug of water.

"While he was sitting there lamenting his hard fate, he heard the gaoler, with his large jingling bunch of keys, unlock the door, and who should come in but his old and dear friend, Pronoun. They embraced affectionately, and Pronoun told him that he could by no means think of letting him remain in that dark, dismal place. 'I should be most heartily glad to be out of it,' replied Noun; 'but it is impossible, for I am kept locked up.' 'I am come on purpose to take your place,' said his friend; 'you must go home to your wife and children, and let me remain here in your stead.' Noun was very grateful for Pronoun's kind intention. 'It is not the first time, my dear friend,' said he, 'that you have taken my place in times of need, but I can by no means consent to your being shut up here.' "

Mary, who now first suspected that the personages of the tale would represent the parts of speech, was very much diverted. "Oh, that is excellent," cried she. "Pronoun wants to take the place of Noun, as it does in the grammar; well, go on, mamma," added she, impatient to hear how the parts of speech would figure in the story.

"Besides," continued her mother, "Noun said that the gaoler would never allow of the exchange. 'As for that,' replied Pronoun, 'we are so much alike that we have frequently been taken for each other. The old purblind gaoler would never be able to distinguish you from me; nay, I dare say, that if I was to stand the trial in your place, the judge would not either.' "

"Yes," said Mary; "a noun and a pronoun are so very much alike."

" 'And then suppose that you were to be transported instead of me,' continued Noun, 'I am to undergo an examination to-morrow morning; and though I am innocent, if the people who arrested me swear against me, I may be condemned.' "

" 'Well, even if it should be so,' replied Pronoun, 'it is better that I should be sent across the seas than you: I have neither wife nor children to grieve for me.' The mention of his wife and children brought tears into the eyes of Noun. 'Ah! my poor wife,' said he with a sigh, 'when she hears this news, her exclamations will never cease. Mine is a very hard case! Well, I will accept your kind offer to replace me for an hour or two, in order to run home and embrace her and my children.' It was so settled, and when the gaoler opened the door to let out Pronoun, Noun slipped out in his stead, without any notice being taken by the gaoler. When Noun drew near his cottage, he heard sad wailings and lamentations. His wife, who was a weak, hysterical woman, had just heard of his arrest, and she was wringing her hands and exclaiming, 'Ah, woe is me! alas! what will become of us? Oh, my dear helpless children!' She was sobbing and crying in this manner, when Noun entered the house; her sorrow was then instantly turned into joy, and she exclaimed, 'Ah! my dearest husband! Oh, is it really you? Bless me! what happiness!' "

Mary laughed heartily at all the wife's exclamations, and cried out, "Oh! I am sure I know her name; it is Interjection: but go on, mamma, I am so impatient to hear what follows."

Her mother proceeded. "Noun embraced her with tenderness, and stretched out his arms to his little children, who ran up to him; one climbed on the back of his chair, and hung upon his neck, another crawled up his knees; the baby cried to be fondled in his arms; and one little chubby fellow crept under his chair, and sat there quite pleased, like a bird in a cage."

"But what were the children's names?" inquired Mary.

"Oh! that I leave to your discernment to discover. What did they do?"

"Why one crawled up his father's knees, another climbed on the back of his chair—oh! now I know," cried she, quite pleased at the discovery. "Up, upon, in, under, are prepositions; so the little children were all prepositions."

"You have guessed rightly," said her mother.

"But they might have been verbs," said Mary, "for they all did something."

"That is true, but I intend them for prepositions." She then went on with the story.

"The neighbours of Noun no sooner heard of his return than they flocked to his house. The first that came were the Adjectives, who lived very near; and after them the Adverbs, who were not much farther off. When they heard that Noun was to return to prison, and to be more fully examined the following day, they all promised to be there to speak to his character."

"Oh! I am sure," said Mary, "that the Adjectives will say he was a *good* sort of man, and the Adverbs speak *well* of him too."

"His wife," continued her mother, "filled a basket with the best provisions her cottage contained; and, before the hour had expired, he took a tender leave of her and his children, and returned to the prison. When he reached it, he asked leave to see his friend. The gaoler let him in; and soon after, let out Pronoun, without distinguishing the one from the other.

"The next morning, Noun was again taken before the justice; the room was full of people; some who came out of curiosity, and others who were his friends, and came to give evidence in his favour. The witnesses were now called and examined; the justice asked the first what was his name, and ordered him to tell all that he knew of the theft.

" 'My name is Verb,' replied the witness; 'I am a farmer, and I was hard at work, ploughing, when I saw Noun come slily up, behind the hedge, under the shade of which several of my sheep were resting. He seized hold of one of them, and was making off with it, thinking, as the hedge was pretty high, that I could not see him; but it was not thick enough to screen him from my sight. Upon this I halloed out in my imperative mode, "Let go the sheep, you rogue!" He no sooner heard my voice than he dropped the sheep and took to his heels. I not only beheld this with my own eyes,' continued farmer Verb, 'but I have brought with me two witnesses who were passing by at the time.'

"These men, whose names were Adverbs, then underwent an examination, in which they pointed out the place in which the theft was attempted, the manner in which the sheep was seized, and the hour at which it took place. In short, they answered every question with clearness and readiness."

"Oh!" said Mary, "these could not be the same Adverbs that promised to give Noun a good character."

"No," replied her mother, "you know, Mary, that there are many different classes of Adverbs. The two witnesses were the friends of Verb, the others were the neighbours of the Adjectives. But to proceed with my story: the magistrate then desired Verb to go on with his relation, and he said,—

" 'As I could not leave my team to follow him, I sent my two boys, good clever lads, who were helping me at the plough, after him, to try to secure him, or at least to find out who he was.' "

Mary, who had been amused at the idea of farmer Verb speaking in the imperative mode, now said, "Oh! the boys were the two helping verbs, To Have and To Be."

"The two little Verbs were then called in to give their evidence. They looked at Noun, declared he was the man whom they had been sent after. The eldest, who was a strong active lad, was then told to give an account of what had passed. He said, 'When father saw the fellow running away, he cried out, *"Have at him, boys!"* We set off full speed, and gained so much upon him, that I thought it would be an easy matter to have him. Indeed I once caught hold of the skirt of his coat, and called out to Toby, who was some way behind, *I have* him; but he gave a sudden jerk and got away, just when I thought *I had him* sure. Well, said I, *I shall have him* again presently, and *I should have had him* before, if my foot had not slipped just as I came up with him. However, I would not give up the chase. *I may have him yet*, said I; and *I might have had him*, if he had not turned into a wood and hid himself among the trees. So then I sat down and waited for Toby, who had a hard matter to keep up with me, and wanted a moment's rest: and *having* taken breath, I *had a mind* to be after him again; but the rogue *had* made clear off.'"

Mary could not refrain from laughing. "I declare," said she, "he has gone through the whole of the verb to have, in the first person; participles and all! I wonder whether Toby will do as much."

"I think one conjugation is enough," replied her mother, "Toby, you know, is a more quiet sort of lad; in his evidence, he said, that the following morning he met Noun going to his work; he then set up a hue and cry of stop thief, and got him arrested.

"Poor Noun had nothing to say in his defence, but that he was innocent. 'If you did not attempt to steal the sheep,' said the justice, 'where were you at that hour?'

" 'I was at work all that morning in the meadow by the river side.'

" 'It is from that very meadow the sheep was taken,' said farmer Verb; 'so it's likely enough you left your work to steal it.'

"All this testimony went sadly against poor Noun, and the justice began to think he must be guilty; when his friends, the Adjectives, came forward, and declared that he was an *honest, industrious, religious, and well-meaning* man, quite incapable of committing a theft."

"I told you they would give him a good character, mamma," said Mary: "I am sure the justice ought not to condemn him."

"A justice does not condemn a man," replied her

mother, "he only examines into the complaint against him; and if the evidence gives him reason to think the accused guilty, he commits him to prison to take his trial at the next sessions, or assizes, when the judges go their circuits or rounds to try prisoners."

"Well; but now go on, mamma, I am so impatient to know the end."

"The Adverbs," continued her mother, "were still warmer in the praises of Noun. They seemed to think that his neighbours, the Adjectives, did not say enough in his favour; for every time one of them spoke of his honesty, or his industry, they cried out, 'Most remarkably honest,'—'Uncommonly industrious,'—'The very kindest of fathers and of husbands.'"

"Oh! the dear Adverbs!" cried Mary; "how good they are!"

"The justice was strangely perplexed at such contradictory evidence; he was quite at a loss how to decide, when a noise was heard without, and exclamations of 'Bring him in!'—'Here's the thief!'—'We have got hold of the rogue at last!' The new prisoner hung back, and struggled hard to get away; however he was forced into court; and he had no sooner made his appearance, than every one was struck with his remarkable likeness to Noun. 'This man must surely be your brother,' said the justice to Noun, 'No, please your worship,' answered he; 'it is true that he is my relative, but only in a distant degree.'

"The justice then inquired the man's name, and he replied, 'Pronoun.'"

"He was not the same Pronoun who so kindly offered to remain in prison instead of his friend Noun," said Mary, "I am sure."

"No," replied her mother, "the Pronouns, you know, are a very numerous family, and he was of another branch.

"The constable who had arrested him whispered to the justice that he had long known the prisoner, and always considered him as a very suspicious character; for that he went by different names, according as it suited his purpose or situation; that he sometimes called himself Relative Pronoun, at others Demonstrative Pronoun, and at others Conjunction; 'but to my certain knowledge,' said the gaoler, 'his name is *That.*'

"The Adjectives, who also knew the man, came forward, and assured the justice that he was a good-for-nothing fellow, idle, and profligate, and the Adverbs confirmed and strengthened whatever the Adjectives said.

"Farmer Verb, who had felt so confident of the guilt of Noun, now began to think himself in the wrong. He owned that he believed that he had been deceived by the resemblance, and had taken Noun for Pronoun. He asked his sons which of the two was the man they had pursued; they hung down their heads, and knew not what to answer.

"The justice then arose; and after having summed up the evidence, 'I will show you the culprit,' said he, stretching out his arm, and pointing to the new prisoner, '*That* is the man.'

"Pronoun, struck with astonishment that the justice, to whom he was a stranger, should know his real name, thought his guilt fully discovered. He fell on his knees, confessed his crime, and begged for mercy. The justice said, that it did not depend on him either to condemn or to pardon him; that he must be confined in prison to take his trial at the next assizes.

"The friends of Noun, who was now liberated, determined to conduct him home in triumph. Accordingly a procession was arranged; two heralds preceded Noun, bearing banners; on one of which was inscribed—'This is a man whom no calumny could injure;' and on the other, 'This is the man who has been so honourably acquitted.' "

"Well, I cannot conceive who the heralds can be," said Mary.

"What is it that goes before a noun, Mary?"

"An article," she replied. "Oh! then the two heralds were the two articles *A* and *The;* and so it was written on their banner."

"Pronoun, the personal friend of Noun (not his roguish relative), followed; and then came the Adjectives and Adverbs walking in pairs, and talking in praise of Noun all the way they went. Farmer Verb and his sons followed at a respectful distance, being ashamed of the error into which they had fallen, and a band of music brought up the rear. The crowd of people was so great, and the streets through which the procession had to pass so narrow, that it often came to a stop; and they would have found it difficult to proceed, had it not been for the assistance of some constables, who had been appointed to close the ranks when they were broken, and to separate those who thronged too closely together."

"Those, I think, must be the Conjunctions which serve both to separate the sentences, and to join them together."

"You are right," said her mother.

"But then, mamma, the Conjunctions—I mean the constables—could only separate the crowd, or join the ranks when they came to a little stop; for do you not know that the Conjunctions cannot interfere when they come to a full stop?"

"They did not come to a full stop, my dear, till they reached the house of Noun; when his children, hearing the sound of music, came out to see what it was; they then ran back overjoyed to say that it was their father coming home with a crowd of people. His wife rushed out and fell into her husband's arms, uttering exclamations of joy; the little ones clung around; the spectators of this happy scene gave three loud cheers, and thus my tale is ended."

After having laughed heartily at this story, Mary began to regret that the lessons of grammar were now finished; when her mother gave her a box, containing a game called the Game of Grammar, which she had made for her, and which, she said, might amuse her, and help to imprint on her memory some of the lessons she had learnt, and enable her to teach the different parts of speech to her younger sisters.

QUESTIONS AND ANSWERS

NOUNS

Q. How are nouns divided?

A. Into *proper* and *common*.

Q. What is a noun proper?

A. It is the name of any individual, person, place, or thing; as, John, Mary, St. Paul's, London.

Q. What is a noun common?

A. It is the name of a class; as, field, house, child, man, table.

Q. What numbers have nouns?

A. Two; the singular and the plural.

Q. What is the meaning of the singular number?

A. It means one.

Q. What is the meaning of the plural number?

A. It means more than one.

Q. Is *basket* singular or plural?

A. Singular, because it is only one thing.

Q. Are *shoes* singular or plural?

A. Plural, because they are more than one.

Q. Is a *pair* of shoes singular or plural?

A. Singular, because there is only one pair.

Q. Are the shoes which make a pair singular or plural?

A. Plural, because there are two shoes.

Q. How is the plural formed?

A. It is commonly formed by adding an *s* to the singular; as toy, *toys*; chair, *chairs*; hat, *hats*.

Q. What are the exceptions to this rule?

A. The nouns which end in *s, ss, sh, x*, and *ch* pronounced soft, must have *es* added to the singular number to make them plural.

Q. Give examples.

A. Kiss, *kisses*; birch, *birches*; lash, *lashes*; box, *boxes*.

Q. What other exceptions are there?

A. In almost all nouns ending in *f* or *fe*, these letters must be left out, and *ves* put in their places to form the plural.

Q. Give examples.

A. The plural of life is *lives*; of knife, *knives*; of calf, *calves*.

Q. Are there any other exceptions?

A. Yes, when the word ends in *y*, with a consonant before it, the plural is formed by leaving out the *y*, and adding *ies*.

Q. Give examples.

A. Fly, *flies;* folly, *follies;* tally, *tallies.*

Q. Are there any nouns which do not change their number?

A. Yes; *sheep* is either singular or plural.

Q. What is a noun of multitude?

A. It is a noun, which, though made up of a great number of individuals, is of the singular number.

Q. Give examples.

A. A *crowd,* which consists of a great number of people. A *swarm,* which consists of a great number of bees. A *flock,* which consists of a number of sheep.

Q. How many genders have nouns?

A. Three; the masculine, feminine, and the neuter.

Q. What is the masculine gender?

A. Every animal of the he kind; as man, cock, bull.

Q. What is the feminine gender?

A. Every animal of the she kind; as woman, hen, cow.

Q. What is the neuter gender?

A. Every thing that is neither masculine nor feminine.

Q. What is the meaning of the cases of nouns?

A. It means their state or condition.

Q. How many cases are there?

A. The nominative, the possessive, and the objective.

Q. In what state is a noun of the nominative case?

A. The noun either does something, or is something.

Q. Give examples.

A. The child *cries;* the horse *is tired.* The child does something, for it cries; the horse is something, for it is tired.

Q. How are the noun and case placed with regard to the verb?

A. The nominative is always followed by a verb.

Q. For what reason?

A. To show what the noun is doing or being.

Q. Give examples.

A. Harry *laughs,* the sun *shines.*

Q. What is the meaning of the possessive case?

A. It means that the noun possesses something; as, *John's horse,* the *child's hoop.*

Q. Explain.

A. John's is in the possessive case, because he possesses a horse. Child's is in the possessive case, because the child possesses a hoop.

Q. How is the possessive case written?

A. With an apostrophe before the *s*, to distinguish it from the nominative plural.

Q. Give examples.

A. In the sentence, "the *cats* are playing," the word *cats* is nominative plural; in *cat's* meat, *cat's* is possessive singular. In *birds* sing, the word *birds* is nominative plural; in *bird's* nest, *bird's* is possessive singular.

Q. What is the objective case?

A. It is the case of the object when acted upon by the agent of the verb.

Q. Give examples.

A. Tom rides a *horse;* Sam fires a *gun*. The *horse* and the *gun* are the objects acted upon, the one is ridden, the other is fired, so they are in the objective case.

Q. And in what case are Tom and Sam?

A. They are in the nominative, being the agents.

Q. Is the object acted upon always in the objective case?

A. No; when it comes before the verb, it must be nominative.

Q. Give examples.

A. The *mouse* is *caught*. Here the object mouse is nominative, because it comes before the verb *is*. The *cat has caught the mouse*. Here the mouse is in the objective case, because it comes after the verb *caught*.

Q. When the object is in the nominative case, of what description is the verb?

A. It is a passive verb.

Q. Give examples.

A. The carpet *is* beaten; the chickens *are* fed. The objects carpet and chickens come before the passive verb *to be*.

Q. In what manner do verbs govern nouns?

A. The verb determines the case of the noun.

Q. Explain.

A. If the noun comes before the verb, it is in the nominative case; if after the verb, it is in the objective case.

Q. Give examples.

A. The *man* speaks; here, *man* is nominative, because it comes before the verb. *Speak* to the *man;* here, *man* is objective, because it comes after the verb.

Q. Are there any other words which govern nouns?

A. Yes; prepositions.

Q. Give examples.

A. Whenever a preposition comes before a noun,

the noun is in the objective case. He went *to* market; market is in the objective case, because it is preceded by the preposition *to*. The parcel is *for* me; me is in the objective case, because it is preceded by the preposition *for*.

PRONOUNS

Q. What is a personal pronoun?

A. It is used instead of the name of a person.

Q. How many persons have pronouns?

A. Three in the singular number, and three in the plural.

Q. What are the three persons singular?

A. *I, thou, he,* or *she,* or *it.*

Q. What are the three persons plural?

A. *We, you* or *ye, they.*

Q. Have pronouns gender?

A. Yes; they are masculine, feminine, and neuter.

Q. Have pronouns cases?

A. Yes; when they come before the verb, they are in the nominative case; when they follow the verb, they are in the objective case.

Q. Tell me the pronouns in the nominative case.

A. *I, thou, he, she,* or *it. We, you* or *ye, they.*

Q. Give examples.

A.   I walk.   We eat.

      Thou speakest.   You or ye drink.

      He, she, or it runs.   They sleep.

Q. Tell me the pronouns in the objective case.

A. *Me, him, her, it, us, you, them.*

Q. Give examples.

A. Come to *me;* follow *him;* speak to *her;* I hear *it;* dine with *us;* sup with *them.*

Q. What are the pronouns of the possessive case?

A.

Singular	*Plural*
My—mine.	Our—ours.
Thy—thine.	Your—yours.
His	Their—theirs.
Her—hers.	
Its.	

Q. Which are the relative pronouns?

A. *Who, which,* and *that.*

Q. Why are they called relative?

A. Because they relate to some word said before.

Q. Give examples.

A. The man *who* spoke; the pronoun *who* relates to the man that was mentioned first. The dog *which* pointed; *which* relates to dog. The flower *that* blossomed; *that* relates to flower.

Q. What is the word called to which the pronoun relates?

A. The *antecedent*, because it is mentioned before the pronoun.

Q. Give examples.

A. The boy *who* coughed; the cock *which* crowed; the rain *that* fell. *Boy* is the antecedent of *who*; *cock* is the antecedent of *which*; *rain* is the antecedent of *that*.

Q. Have relative pronouns cases?

A. *Which* and *that* never change; but *who* has the three cases.

Q. What are the cases of *who*?

A. Nominative, *who;* possessive, *whose;* objective, *whom.*

Q. Give examples.

A. *Who* spoke so loud? It is the boy *whose* voice is hoarse, and *whom* you reprimanded yesterday.

DEMONSTRATIVE PRONOUNS

Q. Which are the demonstrative pronouns?

A. *This, these, that, those.*

Q. Why are they called demonstrative?

A. Because they demonstrate or point out the noun before which they are placed.

Q. Give examples.

A. *This* book is amusing. *That* pen is good. *These* nuts are sweet. *Those* apples are sour.

Q. In what do the relative and the demonstrative pronouns differ?

A. The relative pronoun points backwards to some noun that has been already spoken of and is called its antecedent. The demonstrative pronoun points forwards to some noun that has not yet been spoken of.

Q. Give examples.

A. The *pears which* I gathered; the relative *which* points backwards to its antecedent *pears*. *These pears* are ripe; the demonstrative *these* points forwards to the noun *pears*.

Q. What is a distributive pronoun?

A. It separates a noun of multitude into parts.

Q. How many distributive pronouns are there?

A. Four.

Q. Which are they?

A. Every, each, either, neither.

Q. Give examples.

A. *Every* one of the crowd; *each* of the congregation; *either* of the brothers; *neither* of the two.

INDEFINITE PRONOUNS

Q. What is an indefinite pronoun?

A. It is a pronoun which points out a noun generally, without defining any one in particular.

Q. Give examples.

A. *Some* things; *all* plants; *both* rivers; *one* apple.

Q. Are all the numbers indefinite pronouns?

A. Yes.

VERBS

Q. What are the *modes* of a verb?

A. They show the different manner of doing a verb.

Q. How many modes are there?

A. Four; the *infinitive*, the *indicative*, the *subjunctive*, and the *imperative*.

Q. What is the infinitive mode?

A. It names the verb, but gives you no particulars; it defines nothing.

Q. Give examples.

A. *To write, to speak, to dance.*

Q. What is the sign of the infinitive mode?

A. The word *to*.

Q. What is the indicative mode?

A. It indicates or points out that the verb is positively done.

Q. What is the subjunctive mode?

A. It has some circumstance or condition subjoined to it.

Q. Give examples.

A. I should like to skate if I had my skates. If you should dance, I would play for you.

Q. What are the signs of the subjunctive mode?

A. The helping verbs may, might, should, would, could; and also a conjunction, if, though, etc.

Q. What is the difference between the indicative and the subjunctive mode?

A. The indicative mode is positive, the subjunctive is conditional. In the first, the verb is positively done; in the subjunctive, it will be done only if some condition subjoined to it is agreed to.

Q. What is the imperative mode?

A. It commands or forbids; it also begs and entreats.

Q. Give examples.

A. Go to school. Let him speak. Forgive me.

Q. What are the tenses of a verb?

A. They point out the time of doing the verb.

Q. How is time divided?

A. Into three parts; the *present*, the *past*, and the *future*.

Q. What is the *present* time?

A. It is *now*, this present moment.

Q. Give examples.

A. I speak; she writes; he eats.

Q. What is the *past* time?

A. The time which is gone by.

Q. Give examples.

A. I have spoken; she has written; he has eaten.

Q. What is the *future* time?

A. The time which is to come.

Q. Give examples.

A. I shall speak; he will write; she will eat.

Q. What are the signs of the future time?

A. The little verbs *shall* and *will*.

Q. How many tenses have verbs?

A. Five.

Q. Can there be more than three tenses, the present, the past, and the future?

A. The past tense is subdivided into three tenses, called the *imperfect*, the *perfect*, and the *pluperfect*.

Q. What is the imperfect tense?

A. It is when the action has been interrupted, and has not been completed.

Q. Give examples.

A. I stirred, or was stirring the fire, when John took the poker out of my hand.

Q. What is the perfect tense?

A. It points out that the action has been completed.

Q. Give examples.

A. I have stirred the fire.

Q. What is the pluperfect tense?

A. It shows that the action was completed before some other action was done.

Q. Give examples.

A. I had stirred the fire before you came into the room.

Q. Is the present tense subdivided?

A. No; it is too short to be divided.

Q. Is the future tense subdivided?

A. Yes, into two parts; the imperfect and the perfect.

Q. Give examples of the imperfect.

A. I shall speak by and by.

Q. Give examples of the perfect.

A. I shall have left before you arrive.

Q. What is a participle?

A. It is a word which partakes of the qualities of two parts of speech, the *verb* and the *adjective*.

Q. How many participles are there?

A. Two; the *active* or *present*, and the *passive* or *past* participle.

Q. Give examples of both.

A. Active, *walking;* passive, *walked.* Active, *eating;* passive, *eaten.*

Q. What does the active participle show?

A. That the action is being done, but is not finished; as, *walking, eating.*

Q. What does the passive participle show?

A. That the action is past and completed, as *walked, eaten.*

Q. What have participles to do with adjectives?

A. They are often used as adjectives.

Q. Give examples.

A. A *thriving* child; a *crowing* cock; a *learned* man.

Q. How do you conjugate a verb?

A. You repeat the verb throughout, with all its persons, tenses, modes, and participles.

Q. What are the auxiliary verbs?

A. They are small verbs which help to conjugate principal verbs.

Q. Name some of the auxiliary verbs.

A. Shall, will, can, do, might, let, would, could, and to have and to be.

Q. How do the auxiliary verbs help to conjugate the principal verbs?

A. By adding the participle of a principal verb to the auxiliary verb *to have*, or *to do*.

Q. Give examples.

A. I am writing; he has written; they had written.

Q. Can a passive verb be conjugated without the help of an auxiliary verb?

A. No; it always requires to be conjugated by the help of the verb *to be*.

Q. What is there peculiar in the *cases* of the verb *to be?*

A. The same case is required after the noun as that which comes before it.

Q. Then does the nominative come after the noun?

A. Yes.

Q. Give examples.

A. It is *I* who spoke; now *I* is nominative, and comes after *is*, which is part of the auxiliary verb *to be*.

Q. Can the auxiliary verbs *to have* and *to be* be conjugated alone?

A. Yes, but they then lose their character of auxiliary, and become principal verbs.

Q. What is the meaning of the verb *to have*, when conjugated as a principal verb?

A. It means possession.

Q. Give examples.

A. I have a coat; he had a cow.

Q. What is the meaning of the verb *to be*, when conjugated alone?

A. It means some state of existence.

Q. Give examples.

A. I am a soldier; it is a tree.

CPSIA information can be obtained
at www.ICGtesting.com
Printed in the USA
BVHW04s2002140518
515734BV00014B/111/P